DISCOVERING TRUE WORSHIP:

HOW WE CAN OFFER TO GOD WHAT HE REALLY WANTS

(BOOK THREE OF "ARE WE MISSING SOMETHING?)

BY KEITH DORRICOTT

Ordering Information: Quantity sales. Special discounts are available on quantity purchases by corporations, associations, and others. For details, contact the publisher at the address above.

Canadian spelling used in the text, except for Scripture quotations.

CHAPTER ONE: WHY SHOULD WE WORSHIP?

"Such people the Father seeks to be His worshipers." (John 4:23)

There is something that God cannot give to Himself. Although He is unlimited in His power and ability and provides everything we need (Acts 17:25), He can only receive that one thing from those He has created. And it is what He longs for from us. It is a primary reason why He made us. It is the one thing that should never be given to anyone or anything other than God. That one thing is worship.

How Do People Worship?

There is almost an unlimited number of ways that people in this world engage in worship and religious service these days. For example, Buddhists use an image of Buddha and chant mantras. Muslims recite the Koran and pray to Allah five times a day. Native Americans worship nature, both in the sky and on the Earth. Devout orthodox Jews pray with a swaying motion while wearing a yarmulke on their heads. Catholic Christians worship the Virgin Mary, use relics, and celebrate the Mass. Some Protestant churches have a highly formal liturgy and rituals, while others are very emotional and demonstrative. Some Christian services are very traditional, while others are contemporary. Some use worship leaders and performers. Some have special robes and vestments. Some use prescribed books of worship, while others are spontaneous. Some offer worship services for seekers; others just offer them for the members of the congregation. There is an almost endless variety of what is called worship.

Are these all just cultural differences, matters of personal preference or tradition? Does God enjoy this variety? Does it matter to Him how we do it? Is He looking for creativity in how we worship Him? If it does matter how we do it, what kind of worship pleases Him? How can we know whether or not our worship is acceptable to Him? Again we have to turn to God's Word—the Word of truth—for the answers.

Is All Worship Acceptable?

God cannot possibly regard many of these activities that are listed above as worship of Him (see John 4:22). Worship involves people who know God offering to Him something that He values. The first time the Bible uses the word is in Genesis 22:5 where Abraham, at the mountain in Moriah, *"said to his young men, 'Stay here with the donkey, and I and the lad will go over there; and we will worship and return to you.'"* Abraham was prepared to offer his own son as an act of devotion to God, and it illustrates what God the Father would Himself do years later in offering His own Son at Calvary. It illustrates the essence of what pleases God in worship - appreciation of Christ His Son.

The first people mentioned in history who made offerings to God were Cain and Abel, the two sons of Adam and Eve (Genesis 4:4,5). One of those offerings was accepted and one was not. Presumably Cain and Abel had both been instructed by their parents on how to offer to God, and so it was not just a matter of chance. But Cain did it his own way, by bringing an offering that did not cost a life and was the product of his own labour, and it was not accepted. Abel on the other hand sacrificed a lamb, the best of his flock. This was accepted. And so, right from the start, we see that not all worship is acceptable to God.

Worship is not about us, what we want or what we can do. It is not even primarily about what God has done for us. It is all about God Himself and what He does. The word "worship" comes from the word "worth." Worship of God focuses on His worth and our appreciation of that. Therefore, when we are worshipping, we have to take the focus off ourselves and put it on Him. David, who understood worship very well, put it this way: *"I call upon the LORD, who is worthy to be praised"* (2 Samuel 22:4).

That is the point—God is uniquely worthy to be praised, and that is the fundamental reason for our worship. Therefore, the more we understand Him and His intrinsic worth, and the better we appreciate what He does and has done, the fuller our worship will be.

God wants our worship. He deserves it! And He will get worship—if not from us, then from others. When God's people Israel, at the end of the Old Testament period, was bringing worship to Him that was not acceptable, He said to them: *"'I am not pleased with you,' says the LORD of hosts, 'nor will I accept an offering from you. For from the rising of the sun even to its setting, My name will be great among the nations, and in every place incense is going to be offered to My name, and a grain offering that is pure; for My name will be great among the nations,' says the LORD of hosts"* (Malachi 1:10,11). And then, when the Jewish leaders told Jesus to stop His disciples from praising Him, He replied, *"I tell you, if these become silent, the stones will cry out!"* (Luke 19:40)

Two Aspects of Worship

When the magi came to see the young child Jesus, the Bible says that *"they fell to the ground and worshiped Him"* (Matthew 2:11). This illustrates two aspects of worship—bowing down in humility before a superior being (paying homage), and then offering up a gift to him. In our worship we bow down our hearts in reverence to God. (The Greek word used is "*proskuneo,*" usually translated "worshipped.") We also offer spiritual sacrifices; this is often referred to as "serving" God (Hebrews 9:14; 12:28).

What is True Worship?

When Jesus met the woman of Samaria at Sychar's well, He gave her a wonderful revelation about worship. She had said to Him, *"Our fathers worshiped in this mountain, and you people say that in Jerusalem is the place where men ought to worship."* He then replied to her with this amazing statement:

"Woman, believe Me, an hour is coming when neither in this mountain nor in Jerusalem will you worship the Father. You worship what you do not know; we worship what we know, for salvation is from the Jews. But an hour is coming, and now is,

when the true worshipers will worship the Father in spirit and truth; for such people the Father seeks to be His worshipers. God is spirit, and those who worship Him must worship in spirit and truth" (John 4:20–24).

Christ was disclosing to this woman that worship was no longer going to take place at any particular geographic location on Earth, with "earthly ordinances" (Hebrews 9:10), rituals and animal sacrifices (as it had done up to that point, most recently by Jews at the temple in Jerusalem). These were only temporary symbols, which pointed to the real thing that was to come. But now God was about to institute true worship of a spiritual nature, which would come from peoples' hearts, by means of the working of the Holy Spirit of God within them (Philippians 3:3). Jesus told her that this was what God was looking for—to be worshipped *"in spirit and truth"*—that is, in reality. He was looking for "true worshippers."

CHAPTER TWO: WHAT DOES WORSHIP INVOLVE?

"A holy priesthood, to offer up spiritual sacrifices acceptable to God through Jesus Christ." (1 Peter 2:5)

When Christ spoke to the woman at the well in John chapter 4, He was introducing the fact that true worship does not involve the presence of God coming down to a place on this Earth (as it did in the tabernacle and temple in the Old Testament), but involves us accessing the presence of God in heaven in our spirits, as we looked at previously. We have been given a spiritual nature as part of our human make-up which enables this to take place. In our worship we "*draw near*" (come close) (Hebrews 10:22) to Him through our spirits. Before we explore what this involves, let's be sure about what it does not involve.

What Is Not Worship?

Some people find certain types of traditional worship services boring. Perhaps there is no band (or not a good one) or no entertainment. Perhaps the service is too quiet, and there is not a dynamic sermon. What is it that they may be looking for that causes them to be disappointed? Worship is not for audiences; it is for participants. We are not there primarily to receive, but to give to God. Hebrews chapter 10 tells us that, as we draw near in the presence of God, we must do so *"in full assurance of faith"* (verse 22)—that is, fully believing. We need to be conscious of what we are doing spiritually. If we do not come this way, not only will our worship be ineffective, but we may find it deadly dull. But when we do it in full assurance of faith, realizing the reality of the experience, it will become the highlight of our week. We will realize that we have actually been in the presence of God.

Some people prefer a good sermon to participative worship. But hearing the Word spoken to us is intended for our benefit, while worship is for God. Some people prefer just to do work for God; it makes them feel more useful. But God says that He is not worshipped by men's hands as though He needed anything (Acts 17:25). He is worshipped by us expressing to Him what is in our hearts. That is what He wants to receive from us.

Old Testament Worship

People in Old Testament times never had the privilege that we have today of worshipping in spirit and truth in heaven itself. Their access to God was limited, and their consciences were never finally cleansed of their sin, because the animal sacrifices they offered were incapable of getting rid of sin. Sin is always the barrier that keeps us from God.

Israel gathered as the people of God on the designated feast days in the courts of the temple: *"Enter His gates with thanksgiving and His courts with praise"* (Psalm 100:4). Some of the Psalms in our Bible are from those times. They are "songs of ascents"—the "going-up" songs. The city of Jerusalem is at a very high elevation. It is over 2500 feet above sea level and 3700 feet above the Dead Sea, which is only eighteen miles to the east. As the people came on those feast days, from all over the country and lands beyond, they climbed the mountain to Jerusalem, to the temple, on the pinnacle of Mount Zion. As they went, they sang these psalms of ascents. As they arrived and congregated from all directions, the singing would combine and become louder and louder. As they arrived at the gates of the temple, which was God's house, their songs were thanksgivings for what God had been doing for them. In fact, they brought thank-offerings with them for this purpose. They had entered His gates with thanksgiving, as Psalm 100 says. Then, as they went inside, the courtyard would become more and more crowded, and they would join in singing praises to God for His greatness. They had entered His courts with praise.

However, that was as far as they could go. They were not allowed inside, into the sanctuary, into the very presence of God. Only one man, the high priest, could go in there, once a year on the Day of Atonement, to atone for their sin. When he went in, it was silent. The sanctuary was off limits for the rest of the people. But it is not off limits for us today. In our true spiritual worship we are summoned to come right inside, not to an earthly replica of the holy place, but into heaven itself (Hebrews 9:24).

Certainly God is to be thanked, and God is to be praised. But thanks and praise are not unique to God; they can also be offered to people. However only God is to be worshipped. We today do not have to stop at the courts anymore; we are beckoned to come right into the presence of God, inside the holy place in heaven, because Christ our mediator and high priest is there on our behalf. We are now allowed to go all the way, so that we can give God the worship that He desires!

What Does God Want?

The apostle Paul told the heathen worshippers he met in Athens that God does not need anything from us. He is self-sufficient: *"The God who made the world and all things in it, since He is Lord of heaven and earth, does not dwell in temples made with hands; nor is He served by human hands, as though He needed anything, since He Himself gives to all people life and breath and all things"* (Acts 17:24,25).

However, God does desire something from us. He longs for the adoration of our hearts, the voluntary expression of our appreciation. Although it comes from our hearts, it flows out through our mouths. It is called *"a sacrifice of praise to God, that is, the fruit of lips that give thanks* [makes confession] *to His name"* (Hebrews 13:15). God knows what is in our hearts of course, but He wants us to say it, to tell Him ourselves. And so we do it aloud, we speak our thanksgivings and meditations, and we sing praises together. We are "confessing" to God what we believe about Him and His Son.

So many times in the Bible, when people encountered the very presence of God, they fell on their faces. That is what John did, for example, when he saw the ascended and glorified person of Christ, even though He had been so familiar with Him when they were together on Earth. He fell down on his face *"like a dead man"* (Revelation 1:17). Worship involves complete awe and adoration of our majestic, almighty, eternal God. How much do we know about this kind of worship?

The Lord is not interested in our rituals or the procedures of our own invention that we may go through. He is interested in what is in our hearts. That does not mean that we can be careless in our actions or irreverent in our words, but neither is dry orthodoxy the answer, mere mindless compliance with ritual. For example, the epistle to the Hebrews says that we are to come *"with a sincere heart"* (Hebrews 10:22). Attitude, sincerity, and reverence are all-important.

Worship is not only an offering. It is in fact also a sacrifice, even though it does not involve us giving money or any material things. It certainly does not involve sacrificing the lives of animals, as used to be the case. But it does require serious thought and meditation, as well as preparation time beforehand in the Word of God. Psalm 45:1 describes the process: *"My heart overflows with a good theme; I address my verses to the King."* We do not just come to recite words from a prayer book or to produce lengthy dissertations. We come to express what God has given to us of an understanding and appreciation of Him and His Son. That takes forethought. The words that come out of our mouths should express what overflows from our hearts. This kind of worship will never be boring or routine.

Israel was instructed, *"Three times a year you shall celebrate a feast to Me. ..And none shall appear before Me empty-handed"* (Exodus 23:14,15). Similarly, we should never come into the presence of God without something that He values to offer to Him.

What Pleases God?

How do we make sure that our worship pleases God? For example, is there anything that we know without a doubt really pleases Him? Yes there is, because He has said so, on more than one occasion. It is His own beloved Son. God His Father spoke out audibly from heaven about Christ on two separate occasions, once in the valley of the Jordan River and once on the mountain top, when He was being transfigured. Both times He said, *"This is my beloved Son, in whom I am well pleased"* (Matthew 3:17; 17:5).

God does not speak audibly from heaven very often and so this must be significant. It shows us that when we speak well of His Son, it is very pleasing to Him. And so now it is our turn to tell God that we too are well pleased in Him. When we present our appreciation of the excellencies of Christ to God His Father from genuine hearts, we know for certain that it will be acceptable. And here again, our worship about Christ is not primarily about what Christ has done for us; it is primarily about Him and what He means to God His Father.

What Displeases God?

There are also things that we should avoid in our worship. For example, Israel was commanded not to add leaven or honey to their offerings (Leviticus 2:11). The lesson for us is that we must not mix in with our worship anything that is extraneous to what God commands, even though it might be appealing to us: *"Let us celebrate the feast, not with old leaven, nor with the leaven of malice and wickedness, but with the unleavened bread of sincerity and truth"* (1 Corinthians 5:8).

CHAPTER THREE: THE WORSHIP OF THE HOLY PRIESTHOOD

"So that with one accord you may with one voice glorify the God and Father of our Lord Jesus Christ." (Romans 15:6)

Individually we should be living worshipful lives all the time, as the apostle Paul wrote to the church of God in Rome: *"Therefore I urge you, brethren, by the mercies of God, to present your bodies a living and holy sacrifice, acceptable to God, which is your spiritual service of worship"* (Romans 12:1). Much that we do for God personally is described as being an offering or a sacrifice that is pleasing to Him. But there is more to our worship than this.

Previously we saw that the house of God serves as a priesthood to God—not just individuals serving as priests, but a collective priesthood. We saw from the Old Testament that a primary job of the high priest was to represent the people as a whole. Christ is now high priest over the spiritual house of God (Hebrews 10:21), and He offers to His God and Father the worship of God's collective people (Hebrews 8:3). The unique privilege of being in the house of God is to be able to come into His presence as one people (even though gathered physically in different churches of God in different places). There is no closer relationship to God than worshipping in His presence. It is our crowning experience, and everything else flows from it.

Why Say the "Amen"?

The words of praise and thanks that are spoken in worship are said by various individual men in the churches (1 Corinthians 14:34), as the saints gather for this purpose, but they are spoken on behalf of the whole congregation. The others express their participation in them by saying "Amen" (1 Corinthians 14:16), which means "let it be." Amen is the language of heaven, which is the place where God's will is always fully done (Revelation 19:4). It is also a title of the Lord Jesus, the one who always did His Father's will and gave Him all the glory (Revelation 3:14). A sincere and hearty "Amen" after an expression of thanksgiving and praise demonstrates that our worship is with one accord and one voice (Romans 15:6).

Therefore, an essential aspect of our worship is that it be done unitedly. The epistle to the Hebrews, in its climactic passage that describes our access to God in worship, stresses gathering together to do it: *"Let us draw near ... not forsaking our own assembling together"* (Hebrews 10:22,25). As Christians we may possibly wish to confine ourselves to personal worship and not feel the need to join with others. We may think that this is sufficient and there is no need to be part of a group of people doing it together. Or we may think that it does not really matter with whom we worship. However, if that is the case, we will miss a lot of the privilege that God has provided for us. More importantly, it will leave out a lot of what He is looking for from us.

Is the Lord's Supper Worship?

The Lord Jesus commanded His disciples to remember Him regularly by taking the emblems of bread and wine. In this way we proclaim His death until He comes back (1 Corinthians 11:26). When we do this, we honour Him and obey Him. It is by obeying His commands that we show our love for Him (John 13:35). The bread and the wine that we use are just symbols, nothing more, and yet they are full of meaning. They are designed to help us remember the reality of His body given and His blood poured out, and what they have accomplished. As we take them each time, we are intended to discern in our minds and hearts what they represent. Failing to do this is eating and drinking "*in an unworthy manner*" (1 Corinthians 11:27-30).

We have reviewed how Israel was never allowed beyond the veil (curtain) into the sanctuary, the most holy place, except for the high priest going in once a year on the Day of Atonement. But Christ has now gone into, and is still inside, the true holy place in heaven as our high priest. It says that He is our "forerunner" (Hebrews 6:20), and that He has gone in to appear there before the presence of God—"*for us*" (Hebrews 9:24). That is what makes it possible for us to come in as the holy priesthood—because He is there to mediate for us. He is a man in God's presence—and He is the only one there who has a body!

These verses state that we enter "*through the veil*"—not a physical curtain, but the humanity of Christ, who is alive there. With confidence based on His blood having been poured out at Calvary, and having been applied to us to deal forever with our sin, we draw near. It is these two things, His flesh and His blood, that are symbolized in the bread and wine.

"Since we have confidence to enter the holy place by the blood of Jesus, by a new and living way which He inaugurated for us through the veil, that is, His flesh, and since we have a great priest over the house of God, let us draw near..." (Hebrews 10:19-22).

The way is now clear for us to come before God on His throne. What a privilege!

And so the Lord's Supper, the remembrance of the Lord Jesus, is not the epitome of worship by itself, but it initiates our priesthood worship in the presence of God, whereby we offer our spiritual sacrifices to God through Jesus Christ (1 Peter 2:5).

Is Music Worship?

In some Christian circles these days, it can seem that instrumental music is equated with worship. There are worship bands, worship leaders and worship performers. Does true worship require instrumental music? Back in Old Testament days, instrumental music was an important part of Israel's service. For example, in preparation for the building of the temple, King David organized musicians for the service of the house, as described in 1 Chronicles 25. Yet the New Testament is silent on the subject of musical accompaniment for worship in God's house today. The whole emphasis is on singing from the heart (Ephesians 5:19). The sacrifice of praise is "*the fruit of lips*" (Hebrews 13:15).

The activity of offering spiritual sacrifices by a holy priesthood (1 Peter 2:5) is a matter of presenting to God expressions of thanksgiving and praise by speaking and singing to Him. This is not something that a worship leader can orchestrate; it must come spontaneously from our hearts. When we assemble for this purpose, it is for "*each one*" to offer, as 1 Corinthians 14:26 emphasizes. Hebrews 2:12 shows us that Christ Himself joins in our worship in heaven: *"In the midst of the congregation I will sing your praise."* There is a lot more to true worship than music. Instrumental music has nothing of value in itself to offer.

CHAPTER FOUR: TO WHOM DO WE SPEAK IN WORSHIP?

"True worshipers will worship the Father ..." (John 4:23)

When we come to God to make requests, we pray to Him as our Father, because we're told that He is the one who answers our requests: *"Every good thing given and every perfect gift is from above, coming down from the Father"* (James 1:17). But there is another expression for God the Father that has a unique and very special meaning. It is *"the God and Father of our Lord Jesus Christ."* It is a great thing that God is our God and is our Father, but it is much greater that He has those relationships with Christ. In worship it is His relationship with Christ that matters most.

As we saw previously, Christ's role in our worship is not to receive it for Himself, but to act as an intermediary between us and God His Father. The Holy Spirit's work is to enable us to offer it spiritually (Philippians 3:3). And so the entire godhead is involved when we worship (Ephesians 2:18).

A Very Special Title

Christ often referred to God as His Father, but only three times does Scripture record that He called Him His "God." All three have to do with His humanity—because as a man, He had a God. The first of these was when He came to Earth at His incarnation: *"Then I said, 'Behold, I have come ... to do your will, O God'"* (Hebrews 10:7). The second was when He was on the cross, when He cried out, *"My God, my God, why have You forsaken me?"* (Matthew 27:46). And the third was at His resurrection, when He told Mary, *"I ascend to My Father and your Father, and My God and your God."* (John 20:17). These were three pivotal experiences for Him as a man in His earthly ministry, and each time He acknowledged that His Father was also His God. That involved His humanity.

It is particularly appropriate for us to address God with this title as the God and Father of our Lord Jesus Christ when we are worshipping Him. This elevates our approach to Him, by highlighting His relationship to Jesus Christ, rather than to us. Christ has saved us in order to produce worshippers for His God and Father (Revelation 1:6), because He knew that this is what His Father dearly wanted. Note that Revelation 1:6 refers to "His God,"

not just ours.

The expression of praise, "*Blessed be the God and Father of our Lord Jesus Christ ...,*" is used three times, twice by the apostle Paul and once by the apostle Peter (2 Corinthians 1:3; Ephesians 1:3; 1 Peter 1:3). It is an expression of exaltation and adoration. This is genuine worship.

What Can We Speak to God About?

In Revelation chapter 4 we are told that the apostle John was allowed to see into heaven, and there he saw wonderful things. He saw the majesty of God the Creator on His throne. What could be greater than that? That is the centre of everything. The wonders of God as Creator in all His wisdom and power are a very fitting subject matter for our worship: *"Worthy are You, our Lord and our God, to receive glory and honor and power; for You created all things, and because of Your will they existed, and were created"* (Revelation 4:11).

In the next chapter, John saw something even greater. He saw the Lamb of God, as though it had been newly killed, as the redeemer of mankind, and the only one qualified to carry out the righteous judgment of God. And so even the glory of God in creation is exceeded by the glory in His work of redemption. As far as we know, it did not cost God anything to create this world, but it cost Him His Son to redeem us. We can properly worship God for His great power and wisdom in what He has made, but we can especially worship Him for what He has done in saving us and bringing us to Himself through the work of Christ on Calvary: *"Worthy are You to take the book and to break its seals; for You were slain, and purchased for God with Your blood men from every tribe and tongue and people and nation. You have made them to be a kingdom and priests to our God; and they will reign upon the earth"* (Revelation 5:9,10).

John also saw myriads of angels engaged in worship. Hebrews 12:22 tells us that in the presence of God in worship there are innumerable hosts of angels. Revelation 4:8 tells us that they worship God day and night without rest. Isaiah also saw a vision of the throne of God, in His temple, where he saw the worship of angels:

"Seraphim stood above Him, each having six wings: with two he covered his face, and with two he covered his feet, and with two he flew. And one called out to another and said, Holy, Holy, Holy, is the LORD of hosts, the whole earth is full of His glory. And the foundations of the thresholds trembled at the voice of him who called out, while the temple was filling with smoke" (Isaiah 6:2–4).

But no angel can worship as we can, for we are *"the redeemed of the Lord"* (Psalm 107:2). Angels cannot worship God for their salvation. We will never exhaust appropriate material from the Scriptures for our offerings. The Lord Jesus said that all the Scriptures testify of Him (John 5:39). On the road to Emmaus He expounded in all the (Old Testament) Scriptures the things concerning Himself (Luke 24:27). David said in 1 Chronicles 29:14: *"of Your own we have given You."* The Scriptures are the source where we go for our meditations of Christ; they come from His own Word. But we can only give to God in expressions of worship what we already have received ourselves, and all of that comes initially from Him. That is what enables true worship.

CHAPTER FIVE: LESSONS FROM KING DAVID

"David arose ... and he came into the house of the LORD and worshiped." (2 Samuel 12:20)

David was Israel's greatest king. God called him a man after His own heart (1 Samuel 13:1) because he loved the same things that God loved. He loved God's house, as we saw earlier in Psalm 27. And in the well-known Psalm 23, he said: *"Surely goodness and loving-kindness will follow me all the days of my life, and I will dwell in the house of the LORD forever"* (verse 6). David understood the heart of God, and He understood a lot about worship, even though he did not have the privilege that we can now have. And so let us look at some of the things that we can learn about worship from David's life.

It Is Not About Appearances

"The LORD said to Samuel, 'Do not look at his appearance or at the height of his stature, because I have rejected him; for God sees not as man sees, for man looks at the outward appearance, but the LORD looks at the heart'" (1 Samuel 16:7). When God was pointing out which son of Jesse He had chosen to be king in place of Saul, He passed over the obvious choices until he came to David, the youngest. Others were looking at external appearances—height, regal appearance, and "presence." But God was looking inside at the heart of each of the eight sons. And he chose David, because of what was in his heart.

When we worship, God does not look merely at our actions or listen to the eloquence of our words or the quality of our singing. He looks for what is coming from our hearts. We may enjoy some services more than others, perhaps when there are big crowds, high energy, or good singing performances, but God evaluates on a whole different basis. True worship is not about appearances.

It Must Be Done God's Way

"They placed the ark of God on a new cart that they might bring it from the house of Abinadab which was on the hill; and Uzzah and Ahio, the sons of Abinadab, were leading the new cart. So they brought it with the ark of God from the house of Abinadab, which was on the hill; and Ahio was walking ahead of the ark. Meanwhile, David and all the house of Israel were celebrating before the LORD with all kinds of instruments made of fir wood, and with lyres, harps, tambourines, castanets and cymbals. But when they came to the threshing floor of Nacon, Uzzah reached out toward the ark of God and took hold of it, for the oxen nearly upset it. And the anger of the LORD burned against Uzzah, and God struck him down there for his irreverence; and he died there by the ark of God. David became angry because of the LORD'S outburst against Uzzah, and that place is called Perez-uzzah to this day" (2 Samuel 6:3–8).

David keenly wanted to restore the Ark of the Covenant to its proper place in Jerusalem. It had been gone for a long time. He knew it represented the presence of God among His people. His predecessor, King Saul, had not paid attention to it, even though it had been stolen by the Philistines. As soon as he became king, David set about bringing the Ark back. But he was careless in how he did it. The Ark was heavy, and he used a cart drawn by oxen, the way the Philistines had carried it. David should have known better. God had prescribed that the Ark should only be transported on the shoulders of the Kohathites of the tribe of Levi (Numbers 4:15). It was to be covered and never touched directly. Yet Uzzah touched it while it was being transported, and he lost his life because of it. Uzzah was sincere in what he did, because he was afraid that the Ark might fall. But it was not allowed.

David learned the hard way that when we are dealing with things that are precious to God, they must be done God's way. The worship and service of God is holy, and is not to be treated lightly or carelessly. We are not at liberty to do it just as we think best, however sincere we may be. The church of God in Corinth was warned that they were treating the Lord's supper in a casual way, and they were being disorderly. They were not observing God's divine order (1 Corinthians 11:17-22). God had judged them as a result, causing some of them to be sick and some even to die. They were warned therefore to examine themselves each time before they took of the bread and the cup, to be sure that they were properly discerning their meaning. True worship must be taken seriously.

It is Not For Spectators

"Then it happened as the ark of the LORD came into the city of David that Michal the daughter of Saul looked out of the window and saw King David leaping and dancing before the LORD; and she despised him in her heart" (2 Samuel 6:16).

David finally brought the Ark successfully to Jerusalem. He was so elated at this that he leaped and danced before it in public. He understood the significance of the occasion. But his wife, Michal, who was watching it all from a window, was disgusted at David's performance and thought that, as the king, he had degraded himself in the eyes of his subjects. From that time on, they were estranged from each other. They were not in agreement on this vital matter of the service of God.

David understood that worship is a participative activity. Watching or listening to other people praising God or speaking about God may be enjoyable, and even edifying, but it is not worship. One of the errors that came into the early churches in the first few centuries was the practice of leaving everything to a few people at the front (the clergy, the pastor, or the "professionals"), while the congregation basically acted as an audience. But we have been made to all function collectively as a priesthood, and to all be involved in offering the spiritual service. Worship is not for spectators.

In Good Times and Bad

"When David saw that his servants were whispering together, David perceived that the child was dead; so David said to his servants, 'Is the child dead?' And they said, 'He is dead.' So David arose from the ground, washed, anointed himself, and changed his clothes; and he came into the house of the LORD and worshiped. Then he came to his own house, and when he requested, they set food before him and he ate" (2 Samuel 12:19,20).

Sometimes we may not feel like worshipping God or coming together to keep His remembrance in the Lord's Supper. We may be discouraged or may be going through difficult times. We may be preoccupied with our own problems and may not feel like doing it. But if we allow our variable emotional state to dictate our actions, we will be very irregular in our service. David had just experienced a huge trauma, the loss of his newborn son, due to his sin with Bathsheba. He had pleaded with God to spare the boy's life, but to no avail. When David was finally told that his son was dead, he must have been devastated. Yet His first action was to prepare himself and go to the house of the Lord and worship, even though it was God who had taken his son.

If it had happened to us, we might have been angry at the Lord because He could have spared the boy's life. But not so with David. He immediately went and worshipped, despite how he may have felt. David understood worship.

There Is a Cost

"The king said to Araunah, 'No, but I will surely buy it from you for a price, for I will not offer burnt offerings to the LORD my God which cost me nothing.' So David bought the threshing floor and the oxen for fifty shekels of silver. David built there an altar to the LORD and offered burnt offerings and peace offerings" (2 Samuel 24:24,25). David went up to offer to the Lord in order to stop a plague that had been caused by his sin in numbering the people. He went up Mount Moriah, the same place where Abraham had gone to offer Isaac about a thousand years before. David knew that he was going to the right place, but the site

belonged to a Jebusite named Araunah. Araunah was willing to donate it to the king, but David would not allow it. He knew that an offering to God that had not cost him anything was not of any value. He insisted on paying for it.

So it is with us. Our worship to God is referred to as a sacrifice—"*spiritual sacrifices*" (1 Peter 2:5). There are personal costs involved. It takes time to study and meditate. There may be time or cost for travelling to the assembly gathering. It may in some cases involve ridicule, or overcoming apathy or resistance from others. It certainly involves self-denial in living holy lives, and in confessing sins that we commit. If what we bring to God in worship has not cost us anything, how much is it worth? We must be sure that we are not just giving God our left-overs.

CHAPTER SIX: HOW CAN WE "COME CLEAN"?

"Who may ascend into the hill of the LORD? Or who may stand in His holy place? He who has clean hands and a pure heart." (Psalm 24:3,4)

When King Hezekiah came to the throne of Judah at age twenty-five, things were in disarray (2 Chronicles 29). The temple was in disuse and disrepair. Idolatry was rampant throughout the country. The nation was losing its distinct identity as the people on whom God had placed His name; they were being assimilated into the surrounding culture. The feast days and holy convocations were not taking place. The annual Passover was not being kept. The priests and the Levites were not engaged in the temple service. Nor were they being supported financially by the people as they should have been; instead they were engaged in purely secular activity. The nation was under the constant threat of the cruel Assyrians from the northeast. There had been numerous casualties among the people, and many had been taken captive. Hezekiah's father had tried to compromise with the Assyrians to pacify them, but had failed miserably. The people were disorganized and disheartened.

This was rather a big challenge for a twenty-five year-old. As he took the throne, Hezekiah realized that a massive clean-up was necessary. He organized an intensive sixteen-day work program. The temple and its courts were cleaned thoroughly and repaired. The priests and Levites were restored to active service. But even when he was finished, Hezekiah knew that worship could not take place until cleansing for the people's past sin had taken place. It could not be ignored. And so, on the seventeenth day, he got up early in the morning and made arrangements for something that he knew had to happen first. He gave the command for sin offerings to be offered. The people had sinned, and He knew that, in God's things, we cannot just ignore sins and move on. Hezekiah commanded the people to sacrifice bulls and lambs and goats as a sin-offering to atone for their sins. He knew how important cleansing was before coming into the presence of God. The people had to "come clean."

Today we never need to offer sin offerings. The last (and only effective) sin offering was Christ's death on the cross. His blood cleanses us from all sin: *"The blood of Jesus His Son cleanses us from all sin"* (1 John 1:7). His work on Calvary is sufficient.

Cleansing of Our Consciences

None of the Old Testament animal sacrifices that was offered over the centuries could ever permanently remove the people's sin. The people knew that their sins had been dealt with in the prescribed way, but they did not realize that this was only a temporary covering until the one effective sin offering would be made to take them away forever (Hebrews 10:12). *"Both gifts and sacrifices are offered which cannot make the worshiper perfect in conscience, since they relate only to food and drink and various washings, regulations for the body imposed until a time of reformation ..."* (Hebrews 9:9,10).

But now the single offering of Christ has been made which has totally cleansed our consciences to enable us to come near in worship: "... *For if the blood of goats and bulls and the ashes of a heifer sprinkling those who have been defiled sanctify for the cleansing of the flesh, how much more will the blood of Christ, who through the eternal Spirit offered Himself without blemish to God, cleanse your conscience from dead works to serve the living God?*" (Hebrews 9:13,14). As a result, when we approach God in our worship in the holy place in heaven, we are able to do so because the blood of Christ has been applied to cleanse our hearts forever. Our consciences are now clean: "*Let us draw near with a sincere heart in full assurance of faith, having our hearts sprinkled clean from an evil conscience ...*" (Hebrews 10:22). We no longer have to deal with the problem of guilt for our sin.

Cleansing for Fellowship

1 John 1:9 tells us to confess the sins that we continue to commit: "*If we confess our sins, He is faithful and righteous to forgive us our sins and to cleanse us from all unrighteousness*". This was written to believers, as 1 John 5:13 shows: "*These things I have written to you who believe in the name of the Son of God.*" Since we are already eternally saved from the guilt of our sins, why is this confession of on-going sin necessary? It is because sin of any kind keeps us apart from God. It breaks our fellowship with Him. The only thing that will bring us back into close fellowship again is repentance and confession, and we must never overlook the need for that. We need constantly to be on the alert for sin occurring in our lives, so that we might

confess it and be cleansed from it. This is a prerequisite for our worship and service. *"The eyes of the Lord are toward the righteous, and His ears attend to their prayer, but the face of the Lord is against those who do evil"* (1 Peter 3:12).

Cleansing From Defilement

Even after our sins have been dealt with, there is another problem, the fact that we become defiled in our everyday lives, simply through contact with the world, which is a defiled place. Nothing that is defiled can enter the presence of God (Habakkuk 1:13). Our minds are particularly vulnerable to thoughts that are contaminated by exposure to the world around us. This need for cleansing from defilement is something that we also need to remind ourselves about constantly, about how seriously God regards any taint in the lives of His people. We may tend to become rather tolerant and blasé about it, and certainly the world's standards will not help us here.

We can also become very good at trying to justify our own actions, but the Lord has said: "*To this one I will look, to him who is humble and contrite of spirit, and who trembles at My word*" (Isaiah 66:2). The apostle Paul exhorted the Corinthians: "*Let us cleanse ourselves from all defilement of flesh and spirit, perfecting holiness in the fear of God*" (2 Corinthians 7:1). Constant cleansing from defilement is a prerequisite if we are to enjoy the presence of the Lord. It is very significant that the Lord Jesus washed His apostles' feet in the upper room before He introduced His remembrance to them (John 13:5). As He was doing so He said to Peter, *"If I do not wash you, you have no part with Me"* (John 13:8). He did not wash their feet because of any sin that they had committed, but because their feet were dirty from walking in the world outside. In a similar way, the Old Testament priests' feet always had to be washed at the laver before they went inside the tabernacle or temple (Exodus 30:17).

While sin can only be cleansed by the application of the blood of Christ (through confession), defilement from the world is cleansed through the application of "the water of the Word" of God (Ephesians 5:26). Psalm 119:9,11 says, "*How can a young man keep his way pure? By keeping it according to Your word... Your word I have treasured in my heart, that I may not sin against You*". It is by spending time in God's Word that we cleanse our minds of the natural defiling effects of living in a godless world. It changes our focus and corrects our thinking, as well as making us conscious of any sin that needs to be confessed. This cleansing prepares us for the act of worship.

Defilement Due to Unresolved Conflicts

Because worship in God's house is collective, our relationships with one other are vitally important. Any inter-personal conflicts between us must be put right first. Inter-personal difficulties inhibit true worship: *"If someone says, 'I love God,' and hates his brother, he is a liar; for he who does not love his brother whom he has seen, how can he love God whom he has not seen?"* (1 John 4:20). For example, when the apostles were on their way to the upper room, they had been debating who among them would be the greatest (Luke 22:24), which is hardly the state of mind to be in to keep the Lord's Supper.

The Lord Jesus spoke about what a worshipper should do when he or she is aware that another person is in conflict with them: *"If you are presenting your offering at the altar, and there remember that your brother has something against you, leave your offering there before the altar and go; first be reconciled to your brother, and then come and present your offering"* (Matthew 5:23,24). Personal reconciliation is an urgent priority, and failure to attend to it impairs the service of God. Even though the worshipper in this case was not the one with the problem, he was still expected to take the initiative to get it sorted out. Similarly, the apostle Paul stressed to the saints in Rome the need to persevere in being on good terms with each other for their worship to be effective (Romans 15:5,6).

Defilement Due to Divided Loyalties

Israel's worst sin was not murder or adultery, as serious as they were. It was idolatry. It broke the first commandment: "*You shall have no other gods before me"* (Exodus 20:3). It involved them giving God's unique place as the one who should receive all worship to someone or something else, to a created thing. The worst instance of idolatry was when the devil, who was a created angel, expected Christ, God the Son, to fall down and worship him when he tempted Him in the wilderness: *"He said to Him, 'All these things I will give You, if You fall down and worship me.' Then Jesus said to him, 'Go, Satan! For it is written, you shall worship the Lord your God, and serve Him only'"* (Matthew 4:9,10).

Anytime we substitute anything in the place of God we are committing idolatry, and it is something we must carefully guard against. In the book of Revelation, when the apostle John had seen all the marvellous visions of the future, he was so impressed that he began to worship the angel that had showed them to him. But the angel stopped him abruptly with the words "*Worship God*" (Revelation 19:10). God alone is to be worshipped. One of the evidences of the deity of Christ is that during His lifetime He never prevented anyone from worshipping Him (Matthew 14:33; 28:9; John 9:38). If He had not been God, that would have been idolatrous.

Defilement Due to Conflicting Priorities

But the problem in Israel was not only worshipping false gods. It was that at times they claimed to be continuing to worship God as well. They wanted it both ways, and that is impossible. That is why Elijah said to them: *"If the LORD is God, follow Him; but if Baal, follow him"* (1 Kings 18:21). This practice of trying to mix two incompatible beliefs is called "syncretism." In our commitment to the Lord, it is not enough for us to be doing the right things, such as participating in church services, reading our Bibles, and praying. We must also stop doing the wrong things, things that contradict or interfere. James in his epistle said that a double-minded person is unstable and will not receive anything from the Lord (James 1:7,8). True worship is single minded.

Defilement Due to Misplaced Focus

We may tend to be attracted to things that we can look at and visualize, even in our service for God. But we need to take care that they do not themselves become the focus of our worship. The second of the ten commandments given to Israel at Sinai prohibited any images from being made and worshipped: *"You shall not make for yourself an idol, or any likeness of what is in heaven above or on the earth beneath or in the water under the earth"* (Exodus 20:4).

God knew very well our human tendency to want visual things to stimulate our minds and how potentially dangerous this can be. So He forbade them. The brass serpent, which had been raised by Moses in the wilderness when the people of Israel were dying from a plague, was kept by them. They should have destroyed it, because centuries later it became an object of worship (2 Kings 18:4). It is a natural tendency. Today some churches use relics and images to stimulate reverence. But, as Paul told the people of Athens, God is not worshipped by things men make with their hands (Acts 17:25). He wants to be worshipped in spirit and truth. He Himself is to be our focus. True worship is invisible, but it is very real.

Defilement Due to Reliance on Ritual

Towards the end of the Old Testament, God sent word to His people that He was displeased with their offerings because they were not bringing their best. Their heart was not in their worship, and He hated it. He said to them: *"'Oh that there were one among you who would shut the gates, that you might not uselessly kindle fire on My altar! I am not pleased with you,' says the LORD of hosts, 'nor will I accept an offering from you'"* (Malachi 1:10). Even though the people were still engaging in all the activity, God wanted it to stop. They were just going through the motions. It was not acceptable to Him.

In a similar way, the Lord told the Pharisees that their offerings were not acceptable because they were offering to God money that the law required should have been used to care for parents (Matthew 15:5,6). When we disobey God, we cannot compensate by offering God service. It does not work that way. And so, if we are to "come clean" in our approach to God in worship, we must examine our hearts and our lives and put right those things that will disqualify our worship. True worship is offered by clean worshippers.

> *"Search me, O God, and know my heart; try me and know my anxious thoughts; and see if there be any hurtful way in me"* (Psalm 139:23,24)

CHAPTER SEVEN: TRUE WORSHIP - A SUMMARY

Let us now summarize the main points of this book on the subject of true worship:

- God alone deserves our worship and He desires it from us.
- Not all worship is acceptable to Him. He has told us in His Word what He desires.
- Worship is more than thanking God for what He has done for us; it especially involves praising Him and expressing our awe and adoration of Him for what He is and does.
- Nothing pleases God more than us expressing to Him genuine appreciation of His Son.
- True worship is offered, not by physical means in physical places, but in spirit and truth.
- Gospel preaching, sermons, instrumental music, and good works are for people's benefit, but true worship is directed to God and gives Him what He wants.
- God wants audible worship, speaking and singing aloud what comes from our hearts.
- God does not want rituals. He is looking for genuine, devout, informed confession of His name to Him.
- Our highest privilege as disciples today is to engage in the collective offering of spiritual sacrifices to the God and Father of the Lord Jesus.
- This collective worship is offered by the holy

priesthood of the house of God. The offerings are made acceptable to God through the high priestly service of Jesus Christ in heaven.

- The remembrance of the Lord Jesus in the bread and wine initiates this collective worship.
- Many things can interfere with true worship, such as failure to confess sin, defilement from worldly influences, and unresolved inter-personal conflict. We need to make it a priority to correct these things in order that our worship not be invalidated.

CONCLUSION – SO WHAT ARE WE MISSING?

We have now come to the end of our study. It is therefore time to try to draw together the various strands of what we have been looking at to draw some overall conclusions.

We began by exploring the glorious subject of God wanting to have a house on Earth among men and women, and that today it is intended to consist of people themselves and not physical structures. It is a spiritual house and it enjoys marvellous privileges, but there are also some important conditions attached. We saw that we should not assume, because we are believers in Christ and therefore eternally members of the church that is Christ's Body, that we are automatically in the house of God or that we can share in these privileges. There is more to it than that.

Then we saw that the practical requirement was for an identifiable people to be gathered together on Earth, and we examined God's prescription for this. We explored God's churches, beginning with the first ones in New Testament times, looking for the underlying pattern that He laid down for us to apply today. We saw that they were of God's own design and saints were in them because of His calling, not theirs. We saw again that there are great privileges and important requirements, and that the Lord is quite specific in His Word about how He wants these things done. We should not just assume therefore that any gathering of believers is automatically a church of God, or is part of His spiritual house.

Then we explored the supreme act of service to God, which is true worship. And we asked the questions: "What worship does God consider acceptable?" and "What can we offer that pleases Him?" We saw that more was involved than individual acts of worship, and we delved into the wonder of being allowed to worship together in spirit and truth in heaven itself as the holy priesthood.

Unity and the Truth

In all this, we saw an emphasis on togetherness and collectivity. This does not downplay in any way the importance of our individual devotion and service to the Lord, but it shows the framework within which they should be applied. God is a God of unity. The godhead itself is united, three distinct persons in complete harmony. God always joins things that are alike, and separates things that are different, just as He did at creation. He is not a God of mixtures or of compromise. Independence and isolation are not divine characteristics. He desires all of us as believers, with all our inherent diversity, to be harmonized through the work of His Spirit to become a complete reflection of His own Son, because He is the One in whom His Father gets His full delight.

But God is also a God of truth. He will not compromise His truth for the sake of unity. It must be "*the unity of the faith.*" Otherwise it would be a false unity, a facade. Believers who differ on fundamental teachings of Scripture, or who operate in isolation from each other, cannot function as one. They cannot worship collectively. This unity is much more than an aggregation of individuals, such as separate body parts. It is like a complete body which is operating with all its faculties fully coordinated.

This all has to do with our identity, who we are for God. It is all about our particular relationships with Him, and the spiritual position that we have been given. The privileges and the obligations flow from the position. [1] Neglecting either our spiritual condition or our position results in a relationship that is sadly lacking. We must be concerned with both.

We have seen and enjoyed the fact that each believer is eternally a member of the church the Body of Christ, an indissoluble union that can never be taken away or spoiled. In that spiritual reality, we are one, but we have also seen that becoming a member of it is not the end of our spiritual journey but rather a necessary starting point. The essential point for us is that this oneness needs to be reflected in practice in the way that God has prescribed.

We have discovered that God intends disciples of the Lord Jesus in these days to be gathered together in a community, linked place by place, in full adherence to all of the Lord's teaching for us, as revealed through His Word by the Holy Spirit. He calls those gatherings "churches of God." It was to disciples gathered in this way that the New Testament epistles were written and to whom they applied. It would be presumptuous of us to say that what was written to them also applies to us today if we are not similarly gathered together by God.

How the Body Grows Up

The practical implication of us being members of the Body of Christ on Earth is that we are inter-dependent – dependent on Christ our Head, and on one another. We are each intended to serve a particular purpose, and we have been equipped by Him to do it. We need each other, and we need to be properly connected to each other, in order to fulfill this purpose. If any Body part is missing, disjointed, or not fulfilling its assigned part, the whole is weakened.

How then are we to mature towards this "measure of the stature of the fullness of Christ?" The prescription for this is given, as we have seen, in chapter 4 of Ephesians, verses 11 to 16:

- Each of us is to carefully avoid all wrong teaching, and instead speak the truth of God to each other in love.
- We are to apply this truth to ourselves, and so grow up in Christ.
- As each one of us receives the enabling grace from Christ, we should minister to those we have contact with, also in love.
- We should all aspire to continue this process until we reach a mutual and correct understanding and application of the teaching of the Lord in our lives, and a full enjoyment of every aspect of our relationship with Him.

For us as living members of the Body of Christ to truly aspire to this goal, it is necessary to learn and put into practice the truths from Scripture that we have been discovering.

Knowledge and information about the things of God requires diligent study of the Scriptures these days, usually aided by competent teachers, which God supplies. But what is also needed is a deep heart conviction about these things, which gives rise to a passion to apply them fully in our lives. Even after we have acquired the knowledge, and all our questions have been answered, that conviction and passion can only come from God Himself. If we are sincerely seeking after God's truth, we will earnestly ask for it (Hebrews 11:6).

The Obligation of Revelation

When God shows us a truth from Scripture, it puts us under two obligations. Firstly, it obligates us to live it, to put it into practice ourselves. Otherwise it will be nothing more than a theory. God does not entrust us with a revelation of His truth just so that we might know about it, or to satisfy our curiosity. Secondly, it obligates us to share it with others as we have opportunity, since that is the means that God normally uses to spread His truth.

If what has been covered in the pages of this book is indeed according to the mind of God, then it leaves each one of us with certain inescapable conclusions:

- If the church I am associated with does not adhere faithfully to the full teaching of the Lord, in active fellowship with all other such churches, it cannot be a scriptural "church of God."

- If I am not in a church of God, I cannot be part of God's house on Earth, nor in the kingdom of God.
- If I am not in the house of God, I cannot participate in the collective heavenly sanctuary worship of the holy priesthood, which is the pinnacle of human experience and service today.
- If I am not in God's church, not in God's house, and not able to engage in this true worship, I am obviously missing something very vital in my Christian experience, no matter what else of value I may be doing.

If this is in fact the case, the answer to the overriding question of this book, "Am I Missing Something?" would have to be a resounding "yes!" This may sound distressing, and yet it can be the starting point for wonderful advancement in the things of God. If God does in fact have a particular way that He wants disciples to gather, why would I want to be anywhere else, regardless of whatever natural attraction other places may have? We all have our own personal preferences about things and our comfort zones. And we can so easily make implicit assumptions about things in Scripture, without checking them out to be sure. One purpose of this book has been to challenge some of those assumptions, as they have been challenged in my own life, to force us to examine what the Scriptures really say and really mean. The test of our faith, then, will be our willingness to act on what is revealed to us.

Our natural tendency may be to accept things that are familiar to us, until they are challenged, or until an issue affects us personally. Even then, we can tend to change our beliefs and convictions only grudgingly. We don't normally do it just because someone else tells us to, or because a different point of view is presented. We do it because we have discovered it for ourselves, at a time in our life when it is important to us, when the answers matter to us. Discovering these answers for ourselves can be hard work. There is no shortcut.

Does It Matter?

It is important to keep in mind that these are not just fine points of difference between Christians, debatable points of theology, things that are of secondary importance. These are fundamental issues about who we are and what we do as followers of Jesus Christ. They are of supreme importance to the Lord Himself. We know how He feels about these things. For example, we know about His zeal for God's house, by how He reacted to the money-changers in the temple when they were abusing it. We know how He feels about the church of God, because of how He took Saul's persecution of it so personally. And we know how He feels about true worship, because He died in order to make it possible for us to be a priesthood to His God and Father. The whole subject is at the very heart of the things of God. Paul told the elders of Ephesus that the church of God is something "*...which He purchased with His own blood*" – literally, "the blood of His own" (Acts 20:28).

This book is sent out as an appeal to my fellow members of the Body of Christ out of a deep conviction that many believers today may be unaware of these vital truths, even though they may be greatly pleasing to the Lord in their devotion to the truths that have been shown to them. It is when we are obedient to what we already know that God tends to show us more. There are disciples today who are putting into practice these glorious truths, and who long to share them with others.

If this book causes any believer to examine these things from God's Word, openly and humbly, it will have served its purpose. To that end, I pray: *"...that in all things God may be glorified through Jesus Christ, to whom belong the glory and the dominion forever and ever"* (1 Peter 4:11).

EPILOGUE- WHY I WROTE THIS BOOK

It has been on my heart for a long, long time to try to write a book like this. Not that I necessarily thought that I was the right person to do it, but it needed doing and the conviction just would not go away. Through no credit to me, God has squarely laid His hand on my life, and He has brought me to the point, at sixty-four years of age, where His things are by far the most important in my life, and what I spend most of my time on. This is not to suggest that I neglect other vital areas of my life, especially my family, but I see these as being within the greater context of the Lord's will for my life. Each one of my family is a wonderful gift from God.

I am often frustrated at my failures and ineffectiveness in the Lord's service, but my passion for it is stronger than ever. I am so grateful that He has brought me to a place in my life where what the world has on offer—status, recognition and financial rewards, some of which I have known in my professional career—have fallen into their proper place in the overall scheme of things.

I was brought up in a very godly Christian home and, the older I get, the more profoundly grateful I become for the values, scriptural teaching, and example that I learned from both my parents. I was saved (personally brought to know the Lord) at the very early age of five—and yet there is no doubt in my mind that it was my real conversion. I was baptized and added to the church of God in Glasgow, Scotland, at the age of eight, simply because I knew it was what I should do to be a disciple of the Lord Jesus. At age eleven, our family emigrated to Canada and we transferred to the church of God in Hamilton, Ontario. Three years later we moved to the big city of Toronto, where I have lived in one place or another ever since. We transferred at that time to the church of God in Toronto.

Around age twenty, while I was at university, I went through my first spiritual crisis. I began to have serious doubts about the very existence of God. I never spoke to anyone else about it at the time, although they may have suspected. It was my age of enlightenment, where I was sorting out which of the beliefs that I had inherited were truly my own. The process lasted for several months and it was a very uncomfortable time. But God revealed Himself to me in an unmistakable way.

In 1967, my wife Sandra and I were married, and over the years our children—Adele, Jennifer, and Andrew—were born. I am deeply grateful to God that each of them for themselves has made a deep and lasting commitment to the Lord Jesus, and are serving Him. My marriage to Sandra of forty years has been a hugely beneficial and stabilizing force in my life. She is a very godly, gifted, and caring woman. Throughout my growing-up years, I learned more and more from the Bible, including the teaching of the churches of God that I was part of. I became convinced of it, which is not surprising, given my environment that reinforced it, and I even began teaching it to other young people. Teaching the Scriptures to young people and young adults has always been my passion. Watching the light go on in their eyes as they discover the reality of God in their lives has always been a big motivator for me.

However, in the early 1970s, my second major spiritual crisis took place. There were several men in our church, of varying ages older than me, whom I looked up to. They seemed far more knowledgeable and experienced than I was, and I tended to take what they said without question. But a few of them began to leave the church. I know now that it was largely due to a variety of personal reasons, but I was drawn into some in-depth scriptural discussions about doctrine with two of them. They began to question many of the fundamental teachings of the church, which I had always accepted. I found myself trying to defend these teachings. I was de-stabilized by the whole exercise. This inner turmoil prompted me eventually to begin an in-depth study of these things from the Scriptures, without reference to secondary sources or reliance on existing literature. Those were the days before home computers and electronic concordances, and I generated reams and reams of paper in the course of my study.

What began to emerge was a pattern of teaching that seemed eventually to all fit together. When I asked those who were disputing these things for their alternate explanation of how these Scriptures related to one other, they never gave me one. It seemed that they had a lot more questions than answers.

I was nearing the end of my research when, in a single week, two personal letters arrived. One was from an older brother in the Lord three thousand miles to the west, in British Columbia. The other was from my uncle, three thousand miles to the east, in Great Britain. They had both heard of the unrest in our church and were concerned for me as a young man. The letters were both hugely encouraging, and they came at a strategic time for me. The one from my uncle included a particular offer of assistance, which I decided to take up. I wrote a rather terse letter listing ten key questions, which got to the heart of the dispute, and I asked for something more than the traditional answers to these. Within just a few days a reply arrived, several pages thick, containing a detailed scriptural response to each of my questions. As I read them over and over, I realized that I had been given real meat! It helped me immeasurably. (As you might expect, I still have the letter.)

As the months went by, the Lord again confirmed His Word to me. The other men eventually left the church and went various places. Even though I may not have been able to convince them, I had become convinced myself, and that was what mattered to me. It had taken me to a completely new level, and it bred in me a deep desire that more Christians should see what I had been shown—the marvellous truth in Scripture of the house of God and the churches of God. One by-product of that exercise was a self-study course that I developed, called *Where is God's House Today?* I am convinced that had this teaching not been so seriously challenged in my mind, I would never have come to the depth of understanding and conviction that I did about it, and for that I thank God.

On two subsequent occasions in the years since then I have felt led to re-examine these truths in detail, taking a different starting point each time. On both occasions, I found affirmation in the truth of the teaching, and in both cases my understanding and appreciation of it broadened and deepened. For that reason, I hope it happens again. A by-product of the first of these re-examinations was the teaching video and booklet *Uncovering the Pattern,* which was in use for several years.

While this topic is not by any means the only focus of my on-going teaching ministry to young people and adults, I welcome every opportunity to convey it to other disciples who are willing to consider it. Without a doubt, it is a revelation from God.

The unrest and division that I see among Christians has troubled me a great deal over the years—so much moving about from church to church, without any apparent deep conviction of where they ought to gather; so much disunity among members of the Body of Christ, which can't be solved by "papering over" differences of understanding. I also see it when people from time to time leave the churches of God with which I am associated. In talking with them, all too often they don't seem to realize what they are leaving, and that is sad. There is so much fragmentation among groups of believers today, so many denominations, so many different teachings. We are all members of the Body of Christ—we share that spiritual oneness—but the Lord Himself longed that the oneness might be shown in how we live our lives for Him. He prayed for that unity on His last night before Calvary. And yet these days our culture so celebrates individuality and diversity that we can lose sight of the goal of unity of purpose and unity of service in carrying out all that the Lord has left us to do for Him. As a colleague of mine once said, "We are all accountable for what we do with the apostles' teaching." Even though it is now the twenty-first century, it *is* relevant; it *is* applicable; it *is* vitally important. But it is not well known, and that is a problem.

My on-going study over the years caused me to try to understand what brought about the differences of view and practice that so pervade the Christian world today. This led me into studying Christian history from secular writings, which continue the story after the New Testament leaves off towards the end of the first century. I have found this a fascinating study, full of personal stories of peoples' lives. I have come to be full of admiration for so many of them—for example, for the early martyrs like Polycarp and Perpetua who, despite their limited understanding, were so faithful to their Lord, even to the point of death. And to the Reformers, such as Wycliffe, Luther, Zwingli, Hus and Tyndale, to whom we owe so much. And then to godly men like the Wesley brothers and John Knox, as God was gradually revealing His truth, and more and more of it was being recovered. And then to the young men who founded the "Brethren," such as Darby and Mueller and Newton, who broke away from the established churches so that they could put into practice what they saw in Scripture. And to men like Banks and Boswell who, together with others, rediscovered the profound truth of the churches of God and the house of God and would not let it go. What a legacy I had.

It helped me to see why practices such as infant baptism came in and why it is held so tenaciously by some people; about the emergence of a clergy distinct from a congregation that had become passive; about the insistence on the independence of assemblies; about differences in leadership structures; about differences of understanding regarding certain gifts of the Spirit; and so on, and so on. These all emerged over the centuries, and in many cases they were honest differences of understanding about Scripture. The result is that the Christian world now is a far cry from its early years—there is an almost unlimited variety of beliefs, practices, and churches. And traditions die hard. It is often difficult for any of us to distinguish between the clear teaching of Scripture and a practice that has been entrenched in our minds for a long time. And so the Body of Christ does not yet have "the unity of the faith" that the Lord intends for it. Is there one right church? Does it exist today? Does it even matter? These questions bothered me, but what could I do about it?

At some point along this journey the idea of this book was born. I do not actually remember when it was. The impetus to get down to the effort of writing it has come and gone over the years, but overall the desire has strengthened rather than weakened. Those (very) few people that I mentioned it to from time to time encouraged me to do it.

As I peruse Christian bookstores, read my share of books by Christian authors, and listen to teachers and preachers on television and on CDs, there is much that I enjoy and benefit from. But it surprises me that there is such a void about the aspect of the collective service of God, which is so central in God's Word. Perhaps positional teaching is out of fashion just now, or perhaps it is the way it sometimes tends to be presented, but so much today seems to be only about personal Christian living. This aspect is absolutely necessary, of course, but it is not sufficient. It should lead us to what God is working towards—unity in collective service, things that we ought to be doing together. I have become convinced that all God's purposes are eventually collective, and I fall short if I see only the individual aspects. But we live in an individualistic age. For example, most of the Christian songs that are written today seem to be written from that point of view.

In 1988, while at the height of my professional career and family responsibilities, I was diagnosed with leukemia and told there was no cure. That was to change my life in a profound way over the ten years that I had it. After being told in 1991 that I had about two years to live, and after having had numerous rounds of very heavy chemotherapy (many of which were experimental), I received a bone marrow transplant in 1997 from my younger sister Hilary, after being told by the doctors that it would never happen. However, a year later, with the statistics against me, I was declared in complete remission. Looking back over it all, there was a succession of miraculous occurrences that showed it was all in God's hands. God has also blessed me with good health since then. (I tell the story of my ten years with leukemia in my book *I Want to Live,* which is available from online bookstores.

It became increasingly apparent to me over this whole time that God had unfinished business with me, and I have become increasingly convinced that a part of that business is for me to share this glorious truth that He has showed to me and others. It is in this spirit that I send this book forth, to see what God intends to do with it.

I am well aware that what is written here is not universally, or even generally, held among Christians. If it were, I probably would never have felt the need to write it. For this reason, I fully expect a wide variety of reactions to it. That is not within my control - I am quite content to leave the outcome with God. But I would be remiss if I did not at least try to communicate it to others, and that is what impels me. And so, as Pontius Pilate once said, "What I have written, I have written."

If you have read this far in this personal epilogue, I thank you. I hope that you have or will read this book carefully, referring to the Scriptures noted, asking the Lord to show you what He wants you to draw from it. It is the work of the Spirit of God to lead us into all the truth of Christ. When He does so, it is then up to us to do it.

Keith Dorricott

November 2007

APPENDIX A: THE STANDARD OF TRUTH

"Be diligent to present yourself approved to God as a workman who does not need to be ashamed, accurately handling the word of truth." (2 Timothy 2:15)

As we seek to discover more of God's truth, we need a fundamental standard or criterion to apply. Just as the Reformers applied the expression "sola scriptura", so for us the inspired Scriptures must be the ultimate criterion. But we must properly understand them, which requires that we apply proper principles to guide us as we come to them for answers. Here are some examples of such principles.

The Authority of Scripture

First, we must accept the total authority of Scripture. We must accept that the Bible with its sixty-six books is the uniquely inspired Word of God (2 Timothy 3:16). It is "verbally inspired," meaning that the original words themselves came from God, although they were written down by men. That means that we can be very particular in our examination of the actual words used (in the original texts), and their meaning, within their various contexts.

This inspiration means that the Bible can be entirely trusted to be accurate and reliable, without error in the original. Research into early manuscripts has been thorough enough to give us very strong assurance that the Bible we read today in English and other major languages is substantially without error.

The Bible alone is the Word of God. It is unique. Psalm 138:2 states: *"You have magnified Your word according to all Your name,"* which shows the place that God's Word has with God Himself. The Lord Jesus said: *"Heaven and earth will pass away, but My words will not pass away"* (Matthew 24:35). While there are many other religious books in the world, and also many very helpful books about the Bible, such as Bible study aids, these do not have the same status as the Scriptures. Every other writing, saying or proposition must be tested against the Bible itself. Where it is found to be at variance it must be rejected. This also means that, even although it was written long ago, the Bible is relevant and sufficient in itself. Any fundamental teaching that goes beyond what the Bible itself presents must also be rejected (1 Corinthians 4:6).

Much of what is believed and practised in the Christian world these days is based on tradition. In fact it is an article of faith in the Orthodox churches and the Roman Catholic church that the church traditions may have, in practice, equal weight with the Scriptures. However, not all tradition is bad. In fact, the apostle Paul wrote to the church in Thessalonica: *"So then, brethren, stand firm and hold to the traditions which you were taught, whether by word of mouth or by letter from us"* (2 Thessalonians 2:15). However we must very carefully consider what our traditions are based on. Again, we must apply the test of Scripture. The Lord Jesus criticized the Jewish leaders in His day when He said to them: *"You have made the commandment of God of no effect by your tradition"* (Matthew 15:6 NKJV). He said that they were *"teaching as doctrines the precepts of men"* (Matthew 15:9).

While it can be very difficult for us to change what we have long held to be true, we must come to the Scriptures with an open heart and mind if we are to expect the Spirit of God to show us His truth. Traditions to be rejected are those which have been devised by men, no matter how well intentioned. Traditions inspired by God, as Paul's were, are to be held.

The Interpretation of Scripture

Scripture can only be understood through the inner working of the Holy Spirit. It is *"the sword of the Spirit"* (Ephesians 6:17). Spiritual things can only be discerned spiritually, not just by natural intellect (1 Corinthians 2:14). A willingness to understand them and then humbly do them is the prerequisite. It is not just a matter of academic study.

Even though scriptural truth is absolute, we must be careful that we are properly interpreting it within its context, *"accurately handling the word of truth"* (2 Timothy 2:15). Accurate handling is important because it is possible to misuse the Scriptures (2 Peter 3:16), either deliberately or accidentally. What it means to one person is also what it must mean to others; it cannot be interpreted differently for different people: *"No prophecy of Scripture is a matter of one's own interpretation"* (2 Peter 1:20). Thus, just as the parts of the human body are all inter-dependent and cannot work properly without each other, so the various portions of Scripture are inter-dependent. They cannot be explained in isolation or out of context; one explains the other.

The Old Testament and New Testament

In the New Testament we are told that the Old Testament Scriptures were written with us today in mind, and that "*they were written for our admonition*" (1 Corinthians 10:11). It says: "*whatever was written in earlier times was written for our instruction, so that by perseverance and the encouragement of the Scriptures we might have hope*" (Romans 15:4).

The Old Testament sets out principles and illustrations for us today. God Himself never changes, but how He deals with people has changed from the old covenant to the new covenant. We today therefore take our direction from the New Testament Scriptures. But relevant Old Testament passages illuminate them and tutor us to see Christ and His teaching for us today (Galatians 3:24). When this takes place we find that divine principles are unchanging (see for example 1 Corinthians 14:34).

These principles and illustrations from the Old Testament are particularly helpful on matters that also have application today under the new covenant. The book of Hebrews, for example, makes extensive reference by comparison and contrast to the old covenant priesthood and tabernacle service to teach about service in the house of God today.

English Language Translations

English-speaking readers of the Bible are blessed with a ready supply of translations, thanks to an abundance of scholarship and effort that has gone into producing highly reliable versions of Scripture in their language. New translations continue to be produced. However it is important to realize that even the best of translations include an element of interpretation by the translators. This is because idioms and figures of speech are used, both in the original languages and in the languages into which they are being translated, and so a word-for-word conversion would not be meaningful. In addition, the meaning of words in our English language is constantly changing.

For example, the King James Version of 1611 refers to God having *"a peculiar people"* (1 Peter 2:9), meaning that the people belong exclusively to Him. Today however the word "peculiar" tends to be used primarily in a way which means "odd" or "eccentric". The words *"a peculiar people"* have been changed in the more recent (1983) New King James Version (NKJV) to *"His own special people"* in an attempt to keep up to date with this trend. Extensive research into the original documents over the past two hundred years has resulted in relatively few changes to our Bible. Most of the changes in newer versions are the result of updating to new idiom and expressions.

It is virtually impossible to undertake a translation without introducing implicit assumptions about the meaning of the text, despite extremely thorough attempts by translation teams to eliminate bias. The aim of some translations is ease of readability for the average reader; others aim for precision for the Bible student. One of the most precise versions still available, although it is less readable these days, is the Revised Version, both the English (1885) and American (1901) editions.

In this book, wherever the common English translation of a Bible text could potentially be misleading with respect to a point being made, an explanation has been given for the words which are used in the original language.

The Importance of "The"

One recurring example of translation variation is where the definite article ("the") appears in the Greek text of the New Testament, but is not translated as such in the English, and vice versa. It is a small word, but one which can make an important difference. Generally, the definite article does not appear as frequently in Greek as it does in English, and instead it is often implied. However, where it does occur, it makes the word to which it applies more definite (hence the name "definite article"). We therefore need to consider its use, as it can significantly affect the meaning of a sentence.

An example of this is in Acts 2:42, which the NKJV expresses as: "*And they continued steadfastly in the apostles' doctrine and fellowship, in the breaking of bread, and in prayers.*" Four things are mentioned here, and the definite article is attached to two of them. However, in the original Greek text, the definite article appears with all four of them. It is "*the fellowship*" (meaning a single defined community of disciples), not just "fellowship with." And it is "*the prayers*" (meaning a defined gathering for prayer), not just the general activity of praying. These distinctions are important if we are to *"accurately handle the word of truth."*

The same is true with respect to the omission of the definite article. For example, the NKJV translates 1 Corinthians 3:16 and 12:27 as *"you are the temple of God"* and *"you are the body of Christ."* But the definite article is not in either of those texts in the original Greek, because "the church of God" at Corinth to whom Paul addressed these statements (1 Corinthians 1:1) was not synonymous with either "the temple of God" or "the Body of Christ." They were just a portion of them, and the apostle was emphasizing what they were a part of in order to show them that they should act in a way that was characteristic of them. And so, more correctly, these verses could be translated *"you are* [of the] *temple of God"* and *"you are* [of the] *body of Christ."* Otherwise we may draw the wrong conclusion that the terms "church of God," "temple of God," and "Body of Christ" are synonymous. Therefore the little word "the" can make a big difference to the meaning of a Scripture by its presence or absence.

Distinctions in Meaning

Other distinctions include how particular words are translated. One example is in 1 Corinthians 3:9, where the expression occurs in the NKJV, the New International Version (NIV), and the New American Standard Bible (NASB) *"you are God's field."* Yet the original Greek text for the word "field" uses the word *"georgion,"* which means a "husbandry," a marked-out piece of ground that is tilled and cared for by a gardener (such as the garden of Eden). This is quite different from a wide-open field, where plants grow wild, especially since the symbolism of a field in Scripture is of the world outside (Matthew 13:38). In this Scripture the apostle Paul was not telling the saints in the church of God at Corinth that they were part of the world, but that they were a defined garden belonging to God. Since the very words of Scripture are God given, we need to be careful as to what they actually mean.

"Sola scriptura"

This motto of the Reformers in the fourteenth to sixteenth Centuries, "by the Scriptures alone," was a paramount principle for them. It helped them to break out of the limitations of the church's traditional interpretation of the Scriptures. The statement "*The unfolding of Your words gives light; it gives understanding to the simple*" (Psalm 119:130) was true then and is still true today. It was when people began to have access to the Scriptures themselves, and not just to the church's interpretation of them, and when God's Word began to penetrate their minds and hearts, that the truth of God began to be rediscovered.

Doctrine starts with the letters "do"—we are not just to know it but to do it. Being given an understanding of the Word of God puts the onus on us to be obedient to it. The Word of truth, properly understood, must be the ultimate test of what we believe and what we actually do. That is what we will answer for. Revelation brings its obligations—to live it, and then to share it.

APPENDIX B: WHAT IS "THE FAITH"?

"*Test yourselves to see if you are in the faith; examine yourselves!*" (2 Corinthians 13:5)

When writing to the church in Ephesus the apostle Paul warned them about being "*carried about by every wind of doctrine*" (Ephesians 4:14). Later he wrote to Timothy, using a similar metaphor, about some people who had "*suffered shipwreck in regard to their faith*" (1 Timothy 1:19). The danger he was describing is that believers may be taken off course in their Christian lives and service by wrong teaching. It is just as much a risk for us today, since there are so many different teachings in the religious world, even among Christian denominations. It is quite possible for us to be deceived or led astray.

"*The faith*" is an expression used in Scripture to refer to the whole body of teaching given by the Lord to His apostles, and then taught by them to be carried out. It is the same thing as "*the apostles' teaching*" that the early disciples continually devoted themselves to (Acts 2:42). "*Faith*" is believing something; "*the faith*" is the truth that is to be believed. By the end of the New Testament period, the faith had been delivered to the saints by the apostles in its entirety, and it was not to be added to:

"Beloved, while I was making every effort to write you about our common salvation, I felt the necessity to write to you appealing that you contend earnestly for the faith which was once for all handed down to the saints" (Jude verse 3).

We do not need a new doctrinal foundation today. The original faith taught by the apostles is still entirely relevant and sufficient for us. The faith is described as a "mystery"—truth that can be revealed only by God (1 Timothy 3:9), which helps to explain why it is not universally understood or accepted. The apostle Paul told Titus to make sure that the saints were "*sound in the faith*" (Titus 1:13). He said that some people had "*wandered away*" from it, and that some would "*fall away*" from it (1 Timothy 6:10; 4:1). At the end of his life, he said that he himself had *"kept the faith"* (2 Timothy 4:7). One of the possible dangers of having only a single minister or authority in a particular church is that his own views can become predominant. The counsel of others is often needed to discern the mind of the Lord: *"Iron sharpens iron, so one man sharpens another"* (Proverbs 27:17).

A primary goal for us as living members of the church the Body of Christ is to attain to "*the unity of the faith*" (Ephesians 4:13)—where we as believers in Christ are all faithfully carrying out His entire teaching in fellowship with one other. This unity does not refer to some form of compromise or ecumenical association that ignores or downplays differences of views and beliefs. It is active and willing obedience, based on a full understanding of what the Lord is looking for from us today. That, and nothing less, should be the aspiration of all of us as believers. It is the basis on which we can put into practice the realities of God's house and God's church that we have been looking at. Since it is in fact "the faith," it is vital that we believe it and be fully convinced about it.

Following is a brief summary of some prevalent wrong teachings, contrasted with "the faith" of Scripture:

"Every Wind of Doctrine"	**"The Faith"**
The Bible	
The Bible contains errors. Parts of it are not authentic.	All the words in the original text of the books of the Bible came from God and are totally accurate and reliable. The Bible is unique; all other writings must be tested against it.
Other "holy books" have equal or greater status.	• *"Your word is truth"* (John 17:17). • *"All Scripture is inspired by God and profitable for teaching, for reproof, for correction, for training in righteousness"* (2 Timothy 3:16). • *"Until heaven and earth pass away, not the smallest letter or stroke shall pass from the Law until all is accomplished"* (Matthew 5:18).

The Person of God

There is no god. There are many gods. Everything is god. Jesus Christ was not eternally God the Son. The Holy Spirit is just an influence, not a person of the godhead.	There is one true and living God, in three persons—Father, Son (Jesus Christ), and Holy Spirit. • *"There is one God."* (1 Timothy 2:5). • *"The Lord is the true God; He is the living God and the everlasting King"* (Jeremiah 10:10). • *"In the beginning was the Word, and the Word was with God, and the Word was God"* (John 1:1), referring to Christ. • *"Jesus the Son of God"* (Hebrews 4:14). • *"Ananias, why has Satan filled your heart to lie to the Holy Spirit ... you have not lied to men but to God"* (Acts 5:3,4).

Salvation

People are saved by their own good life, where the good outweighs the bad. Believers can lose their salvation. God will not punish unbelievers eternally.	Salvation is by faith alone, by God's grace. It is eternally secure. Those not saved will face God's eternal punishment. • *"For by grace you have been saved through faith; and that not of yourselves, it is the gift of God"* (Ephesians 2:8). • *"I give eternal life to them, and they will never perish"* (John 10:28). • *"These will go away into eternal punishment, but the righteous into eternal life"* (Matthew 25:46). • *"He who believes in the Son has eternal life; but he who does not obey the Son will not see life, but the wrath of God abides on him"* (John 3:36).

The Work of the Holy Spirit

Miraculous gifts of the Spirit still apply today.

All believers should pray to be baptized by the Holy Spirit as a second blessing, and speak in tongues (unknown languages).

Miraculous gifts (such as the ability to speak in unknown languages and to heal people) were given to some believers in the early days of the apostles to validate their new teaching, before the New Testament Scriptures were complete. Believers are baptized "in" (not "by") the Holy Spirit at the time of their salvation. Thereafter they are exhorted to be filled with the Spirit. Tongues were only used as a sign of the giving of the Holy Spirit in new circumstances (Acts 2:4;10:46;19:6). Otherwise, during the apostolic period, they were to be used very selectively, and only with an interpreter (1 Corinthians 14:5).

- *"After it was at the first spoken through the Lord, it was confirmed to us by those who heard, God also testifying with them, both by signs and wonders and by various miracles and by gifts of the Holy Spirit according to His own will"* (Hebrews 2:3,4).
- *"By one Spirit we were all*

baptized into one body" (1 Corinthians 12:13).

- *"Be filled with the Spirit"* (Ephesians 5:18).
- *"All do not have gifts of healings, do they? All do not speak with tongues, do they?"* (1 Corinthians 12:30)

Baptism

Baptism is necessary for salvation.

Sprinkling is an acceptable alternative to immersion.

Infants should be baptized (sprinkled, "christened").

Baptism is optional for a disciple.

Baptism need not be into the name of the Father and of the Son and of the Holy Spirit.

Salvation is by faith alone.

- *"For by grace you have been saved through faith; and that not of yourselves, it is the gift of God not as a result of works, so that no one may boast"* (Ephesians 2:8,9).
- *"Therefore, having been justified by faith, we have peace with God through our Lord Jesus Christ"* (Romans 5:1).

Baptism is a public testimony to our salvation.

- *"So then, those who had received his word were baptized"* (Acts 2:41).

Jesus was baptized, although He did not need salvation.

- *"Jesus answering said to him, 'Permit it at this time; for in this way it is fitting for us to fulfill all righteousness.' Then he permitted Him. After being baptized, Jesus came up immediately from the water*" (Matthew 3:15,16).

Baptism is by immersion in water. It symbolizes being identified with the burial and resurrection of Christ.

- "*He ordered the chariot to stop; and they both went down into the water, Philip as well as the eunuch, and he baptized him. When they came up out of the water, the Spirit of the Lord snatched Philip away*" (Acts 8:38,39).
- "*Do you not know that all of us who have been baptized into Christ Jesus have been baptized into His death? Therefore we have been buried with Him through baptism into death, so that as Christ was raised from the dead through the glory of the Father, so we too might walk in newness of life*" (Romans

6:3,4).

Believers are commanded to be baptized; it requires a response of obedience.

- "*He ordered them to be baptized in the name of Jesus Christ*" (Acts 10:48).

The Lord instructed His apostles to baptize disciples into the name of the Father and of the Son and of the Holy Spirit.

- "*Go therefore and make disciples of all the nations, baptizing them in* [Greek "eis": into] *the name of the Father and the Son and the Holy Spirit*" (Matthew 28:19).

Church Gathering

Believers are free to worship wherever and however they choose.

All believers are in the priesthood.

Salvation is the only requirement for church membership and for keeping the Lord's Supper.

Believers and unbelievers can worship together.

God has prescribed churches of God where baptized disciples should be added.

- "*To the church of God which is at Corinth, to those who have been sanctified in Christ Jesus, saints by calling...*" (1 Corinthians 1:2).
- "*So then, those who had received his word were baptized; and that day there were added about three thousand souls*" (Acts 2:41).

God "calls" disciples into "the fellowship of His Son," a community of disciples committed to unitedly carrying out the Lord's commands as taught by His apostles.

- "*God is faithful, by whom you were called into the fellowship of His Son, Jesus Christ our Lord*" (1 Corinthians 1:9 NKJV).

This community constitutes the house of God, where those disciples who have been built into it can worship God as a holy priesthood. Unbelievers, unbaptized believers, and believers not added to a church of God do not have this privilege.

- "*So then you are no longer strangers and aliens, but you are fellow citizens with the saints, and are of God's household, having been built on the foundation of the apostles and prophets, Christ Jesus Himself being the corner stone, in whom the whole building, being fitted together, is growing into a holy temple in the Lord, in whom you also are being built together into a dwelling of God in the Spirit*" (Ephesians 2:19-22).
- "*You also, as living stones, are being built up as a spiritual house for a holy priesthood, to offer up spiritual sacrifices acceptable to God through Jesus Christ*" (1 Peter 2:5).
- "*John to the seven churches that are in Asia...To Him who*

loves us and released us from our sins by His blood - and He has made us to be a kingdom, priests to His God and Father" (Revelation 1:4-6).

Leadership

Apostles should be appointed today.

Apostles of the Lord Jesus were men who had seen Him and received their teaching directly from Him, and so there can be no apostles today.

- "*Am I not an apostle? Have I not seen Jesus our Lord?*" (1 Corinthians 9:1)
- "*I received from the Lord that which I also delivered to you*" (1 Corinthians 11:23).

Since only apostles can appoint elders and there are not any apostles today, elders should not be appointed.

The apostle Paul instructed Titus (not an apostle) to appoint elders.

- "*For this reason I left you in Crete, that you would set in order what remains and appoint elders in every city as I directed you*" (Titus 1:5).

Clergy should be appointed to carry out the service of the church.

Elders are "among" the saints.

- "*I exhort the elders among you, as your fellow elder... shepherd the flock of God among you*" (1 Peter 5:1,2).

Women may undertake leadership roles.

All the saints in a church of God

should actively engage in its service.

- "*When you assemble, each one has a psalm, has a teaching, has a revelation, has a tongue, has an interpretation. Let all things be done for edification*" (1 Corinthians 14:26).

Women are not to exercise authority over men in the church.

- "*I do not allow a woman to teach or exercise authority over a man, but to remain quiet*" (1 Timothy 2:12).

Each church can be independent of others.

Churches of God are to follow the same teaching, and support each other. Their elders should be united.

- "*So I direct in all the churches*" (1 Corinthians 7:17).
- "*When Paul and Barnabas had great dissension and debate with them, the brethren determined that Paul and Barnabas and some others of them should go up to Jerusalem to the apostles and*

elders concerning this issue" (Acts 15:2).

- "*While they were passing through the cities, they were delivering the decrees which had been decided upon by the apostles and elders who were in Jerusalem, for them to observe. So the churches were being strengthened in the faith, and were increasing in number daily*" (Acts 16:4,5).

APPENDIX C: COMMENTS ON SELECTED SCRIPTURES

Many New Testament Scriptures have been referred to throughout this book. Some of these are particularly relevant to establishing the spiritual position of disciples of the Lord Jesus in (a) the church the Body of Christ, (b) the house of God, and (c) churches of God. Following is a fuller commentary on these aspects of some of these passages, in their context.

Matthew 28:18–20

"And Jesus came up and spoke to them, saying, 'All authority has been given to Me in heaven and on earth. Go therefore and make disciples of all the nations, baptizing them in the name of the Father and the Son and the Holy Spirit, teaching them to observe all that I commanded you; and lo, I am with you always, even to the end of the age.'"

This was one of the Lord's final acts on Earth before He ascended to heaven. In it He announced that God had given Him total authority, both in heavenly realms (1 Peter 3:22) and throughout the Earth. The apostle Peter preached that Jesus is Lord a few days later at Pentecost (Acts 2:36). When a person becomes a disciple, Jesus does not become their Lord; He is already Lord of all (Acts 10:36). The person is acknowledging the fact that He is their Lord and is willingly subjecting themselves to Him.

Jesus then gave them what is often referred to as the "Great Commission." The apostles were to go and make disciples of all nationalities. The gospel was to be worldwide (although it was restricted initially to the Jews). Making a disciple is more than telling people to believe in Jesus Christ for eternal life; it also involves bringing them to the point of submitting themselves to follow Him as Lord. They were to baptize and teach those disciples. In fact, the wording shows that the baptizing and teaching were an integral part of making them disciples—literally "*make disciples, baptizing and teaching them.*" There is no support given in Scripture for the notion of believing for salvation but not also following as a disciple.

The baptism was to be "*into*" (Greek: *eis*) the name (singular) of the Father and the Son and the Holy Spirit. A person is baptized (immersed) "*by*" another disciple, "*in*" water, "*into*" that name (indicating the deity and authority of the Lord Jesus Christ). [2] These words "*into the name of the Father and of the Son and of the Holy Spirit*" are not repeated in subsequent references to disciples' baptism in the book of Acts. However the fact that it is so explicit in this first mention by the Lord Himself, and carries such significance, shows that this is how it should be done today.

Acts 1:1–5

"The first account I composed, Theophilus, about all that Jesus began to do and teach, until the day when He was taken up to heaven, after He had by the Holy Spirit given orders to the apostles whom He had chosen. To these He also presented Himself

alive after His suffering, by many convincing proofs, appearing to them over a period of forty days and speaking of the things concerning the kingdom of God. Gathering them together, He commanded them not to leave Jerusalem, but to wait for what the Father had promised, 'Which,' He said, 'you heard of from Me; for John baptized with water, but you will be baptized with the Holy Spirit not many days from now.'"

This forty-day period that the Lord Jesus spent on Earth with His eleven apostles, between His resurrection and His ascension to heaven, was an intense time of learning for them. He was preparing them for the task of carrying on His work in His absence. He gave them commandments to keep, and He instructed them to teach them all to the new disciples who would believe through their word (Matthew 28:20; John 17:20). We are not told explicitly what He said, but we can deduce it clearly from what they did after He left.

The overall subject was the kingdom of God. The kingdom had been taken away from the nation of Israel, because of their disobedience (Matthew 21:43). He was now about to give it to them and to those joined with them, at Pentecost, as the "little flock" (Luke 12:32). After His departure, that is what they preached and taught—"the kingdom of God"—as the book of Acts describes throughout. It was how disciples were to live and serve together, keeping all that the Lord had commanded. At the end of the book of Acts the apostle Paul was in Rome still "*preaching the kingdom of God and teaching concerning the Lord Jesus Christ*" (Acts 28:31).

The power within them in carrying out this commission was to be the Holy Spirit, which God was about to pour out on them and others, beginning at Pentecost. They were not to begin this work until they received Him. This was not a work they could do on their own.

Acts 2:41–47

"So then, those who had received his word were baptized; and that day there were added about three thousand souls. They were continually devoting themselves to the apostles' teaching and to fellowship, to the breaking of bread and to prayer. Everyone kept feeling a sense of awe; and many wonders and signs were taking place through the apostles. And all those who had believed were together and had all things in common; and they began selling their property and possessions and were sharing them with all, as anyone might have need. Day by day continuing with one mind in the temple, and breaking bread from house to house, they were taking their meals together with gladness and sincerity of heart, praising God and having favor with all the people. And the Lord was adding to their number day by day those who were being saved."

The hundred and twenty or so disciples had been waiting in Jerusalem for the Holy Spirit to come (Acts 1:15), as the Lord Jesus had promised them. Jerusalem was the place where He had so recently been crucified, and where His grave was, which was now empty. It was where the great temple was, which was being replaced as where God would be worshipped by His people. They were "*all together in one place*" (verse 1), called to be there by the Lord Himself, for one purpose. In effect, they were a church, although that word is not used. That is what a church is, a collection of people called out by God from wherever they were to be together for Him. However, they were about to become "the church of God in Jerusalem" with the arrival of the Holy Spirit.

The pouring out of the Spirit gave Peter his opportunity (and also the ability) to preach the gospel to the devout Jews who came to investigate. About three thousand of them responded to His preaching—they *"gladly received"* (NKJV) his word. They were all baptized and added to those who were already together. The formula of Matthew 28:19,20 was being carried out. The result was that on that day two divine things came into existence—the church the Body of Christ, that the Lord had spoken about in Matthew 16:18, and the church of God in Jerusalem. Those people became part of both of them, which is of course the ideal. However, that situation did not last, because being in a church of God requires on-going adherence to the Lord's teaching, while being in the Body does not.

The three things that are mentioned in verse 41 happened to each of them as individuals, and only need to happen once for each person—salvation, water baptism, and addition to a church of God. But they need to happen in that sequence. And then verse 42 describes four things that the church was *"devoting themselves to"* (or "*continuing steadfastly in*" NKJV), that happened continually and were done collectively. Again the sequence is important. They continued in "the apostles teaching"—that is, they were taught and were obedient to what the Lord Jesus had taught the apostles during the forty days, as referred to in Acts 1:1–5. They also continued in the fellowship of the apostles and others; they were a community. They did not stay together and then decide what the teaching would be; they became in effect a partnership based on their common adherence to the full teaching. The teaching came first. That community was described later by the apostle Paul as "*the fellowship of His Son, Jesus Christ our Lord*" (1 Corinthians 1:9). Then it says that they continued in "the breaking of bread" (the remembrance of the Lord Jesus with the bread and wine, as He had commanded in Luke 22:19), and in "the prayers" (the gatherings for collective prayer, such as is recorded in Acts 12:5). These four things were vitally important and definitely worth devoting themselves to.

As noted in Appendix A, all four of these activities include the definite article. "The apostles' teaching" was a single body of doctrine. "The fellowship" was a single defined community. "The breaking of bread" was a regular defined service, distinct from "breaking bread" as in verse 46 (which refers to taking meals together). "The prayers" was a regular defined gathering for prayer by the church, distinct from praying individually or in informal groups. These seven steps in verses 41 and 42, in their proper order, set a pattern for us to follow today.

Acts 14:21–23

"After they had preached the gospel to that city and had made many disciples, they returned to Lystra and to Iconium and to Antioch, strengthening the souls of the disciples, encouraging them to continue in the faith, and saying, 'Through many tribulations

we must enter the kingdom of God.' When they had appointed elders for them in every church, having prayed with fasting, they commended them to the Lord in whom they had believed."

In his missionary journeys, the apostle Paul not only covered new territory, he often re-visited existing churches to strengthen them. Discipleship is an on-going matter and it requires continual support and building up. This is why he returned at this particular time to the three churches in these towns in the southern part of Asia Minor. In these verses we see the link that exists between: (a) "the faith" (the commands of the Lord; the apostles' teaching); (b) "the kingdom of God," the community where that teaching was practiced; (c) the "church" in each of those places, consisting of gatherings of disciples there; and (d) "elders," who had the God-given responsibility to care for those churches (1 Timothy 3:5).

Romans 6:17

"But thanks be to God that though you were slaves of sin, you became obedient from the heart to that form of teaching to which you were committed."

In Jude verse 3 we are told that the faith (the Lord's teaching for His disciples today) had been fully delivered to the saints. In this Scripture the reverse picture is given. Paul describes the saints as having been delivered to the doctrine. He describes it as a form, a mould or pattern, that they were being poured into. It would shape their lives and their service. Not only was the teaching delivered to them to keep, they were also delivered to it and must conform to it.

1 Corinthians 1:1,2,9

"Paul, called as an apostle of Jesus Christ by the will of God, and Sosthenes our brother, to the church of God which is at Corinth, to those who have been sanctified in Christ Jesus, saints by calling, with all who in every place call on the name of our Lord Jesus Christ, their Lord and ours: ... God is faithful, through whom you were called into fellowship with His Son, Jesus Christ our Lord."

In these three verses at the start of his first letter to the church at Corinth, the apostle Paul used the word "call" four times, with various meanings. (Variants of the word are used in the original Greek text.)

Firstly, he told those in the church that God had called him to be an apostle; that was his own unique calling to his life-work. Secondly, he told them that God had called them (summoned them, appointed them) to be "saints" (holy ones, set apart for God). This applied equally to all of them. Thirdly, he linked them with others in various places who "call on" the name of the Lord. This is a general term used quite widely in the Bible to refer to worshipping, praying, and responding to the Lord. It is used to refer to the church in Jerusalem when Paul himself was persecuting them (Acts 9:14). Finally he told them that God had called them into "the fellowship" of His Son, the community of those who were gathered in the same way as they were, in churches of God.

It was clear that those in the church were not just there by their own choice. They had responded to the call (summons) of God through the proclamation of His Word. They had been called into that local church, but also into the wider community. The definite article is present before the word "fellowship" in verse 9. It was a defined fellowship (partnership, community) belonging to the Lord Jesus, such as was referred to in Acts 2:42. It is not identical to fellowship "with" God as described in 1 John 1:3, although it certainly includes that.

1 Corinthians 3:9–17

"For we are God's fellow workers; you are God's field, God's building. According to the grace of God which was given to me, like a wise master builder I laid a foundation, and another is building on it. But each man must be careful how he builds on it. For no man can lay a foundation other than the one which is laid, which is Jesus Christ. Now if any man builds on the foundation with gold, silver, precious stones, wood, hay, straw, each man's work will become evident; for the day will show it because it is to be revealed with fire, and the fire itself will test the quality of each man's work. If any man's work which he has built on it remains, he will receive a reward. If any man's work is burned up, he will suffer loss; but he himself will be saved, yet so as through fire. Do you not know that you are a temple of God and that the Spirit of God dwells in you? If any man destroys the temple of God, God will destroy him, for the temple of God is holy, and that is what you are."

Here the apostle Paul is describing how the church of God in Corinth came into existence (as recorded in Acts 18:1–11). His primary role as an apostle there, as everywhere else, was to lay the foundation teaching about Christ. This was the apostles' teaching and it had to correspond entirely to the heavenly reality of Christ's position in heaven as the foundation stone of the spiritual house of God (1 Peter 2:6). Once the foundational teaching was established, it never needed to be amended or added to, but others in the church were to build on that by putting it into practice in their service for God. He warned them all that their works would be evaluated one day, and those would prove to have been positive ("gold, silver, or precious stones"), or worthless ("wood, hay, stubble"). The works may even be destructive (verse 17), for which there would be judgment. In verse 9 he described the church in Corinth as a building—not a physical building, of course, but what God was building in that city. It is a metaphor he also used later in Ephesians 2:21.

Then to the church he said, *"Do you not know that you are the temple of God?"* (verse 16). The definite article is not in the original text; literally it reads, "*You are temple of God.*" The expression "temple of God" is another term for the house of God. The church of God in Corinth was not the whole house, of course, but they were part of it and they were expected to reflect its character of holiness.

1 Corinthians 11:18–26

"For, in the first place, when you come together as a church, I hear that divisions exist among you; and in part I believe it. For there must also be factions among you, so that those who are approved may become evident among you. Therefore when you meet together, it is not to eat the Lord's Supper, for in your eating each one takes his own supper first; and one is hungry and another is drunk. What! Do you not have houses in which to eat and

drink? Or do you despise the church of God and shame those who have nothing? What shall I say to you? Shall I praise you? In this I will not praise you.

For I received from the Lord that which I also delivered to you, that the Lord Jesus in the night in which He was betrayed took bread; and when He had given thanks, He broke it and said, 'This is My body, which is for you; do this in remembrance of Me.' In the same way He took the cup also after supper, saying, 'This cup is the new covenant in My blood; do this, as often as you drink it, in remembrance of Me.' For as often as you eat this bread and drink the cup, you proclaim the Lord's death until He comes."

Paul is here correcting disorder in how the church was keeping the remembrance of the Lord Jesus, the Lord's Supper. It appears that they were treating it as a social event and, with the cliques that existed among them (1:10,11), they were acting very independently of one another and without proper regard for what the occasion meant. It was so serious that some of their number were sick and some had died, as a result of the Lord's judgment on them. Paul indicates that he obtained this teaching about the Lord's Supper directly from the Lord Jesus Himself (rather than from one of the other apostles who had been there in person on the night that the Lord instituted it). Paul makes it clear that the saints were to gather as a church for this remembrance, and not just as individuals. Their unity of heart and practice was vital. By acting as they had been doing, they had despised God's church, treating of little value something that was extremely precious to Him. It may only have been the actions of some of them, but they were a unit and it reflected on them all.

2 Corinthians 6:14–18

"Do not be bound together with unbelievers; for what partnership have righteousness and lawlessness, or what fellowship has light with darkness? Or what harmony has Christ with Belial, or what has a believer in common with an unbeliever? Or what agreement has the temple of God with idols? For we are the temple of the living God; just as God said, 'I will dwell in them and walk among them; and I will be their God, and they shall be My people. Therefore, come out from their midst and be separate,' says the Lord. 'And do not touch what is unclean; and I will welcome you. And I will be a father to you, and you shall be sons and daughters to Me,' says the Lord Almighty."

Here, in his second letter to the church at Corinth, Paul was correcting the problem of their lack of separation from people who did not believe and practice God's truth. He told them that they could not keep their identity as God's people unless they came out from things that were opposed to it. There is no room for mixing truth with error, righteousness with unrighteousness, and the house of God with idolatry. They were being defiled by joining with what was not of God, and they needed to be cleansed of it. Because he was addressing them as a church of God (2 Corinthians 1:1), he shows that there is a clear link between it and the temple of God and the people of God (verse 16).

If they would respond positively to this warning, he states, they would enjoy the presence of God in them [3] collectively as His own people, and He would treat them as His "sons and daughters" living with Him in His house. This was something beyond their relationship with Christ in the church which is His Body, in which there are no gender distinctions of sons and daughters (Galatians 3:28). The expression *"walk among them"* is reminiscent of the vision that John saw later of the Lord Jesus walking among the seven churches (Revelation 2:1).

Ephesians 2:19–22

"So then you are no longer strangers and aliens, but you are fellow citizens with the saints, and are of God's household, having been built on the foundation of the apostles and prophets, Christ Jesus Himself being the corner stone, in whom the whole building, being fitted together, is growing into a holy temple in the Lord, in whom you also are being built together into a dwelling of God in the Spirit."

In this chapter, the apostle Paul describes what had happened to the Gentile (non-Jewish) saints in the church in Ephesus. He starts the chapter by describing them before their salvation, when they had been *"dead in your trespasses and sins,"* and finishes the chapter with them being *"a dwelling of God in the Spirit."* What a transformation! In these final four verses, He uses the following expressions to describe them:

- *"Fellow citizens with the saints"*—they had equal status with Jewish disciples, something they had never enjoyed in Old Testament times.
- *"Of God's household"*—they were part of the spiritual house, living stones built into it.
- *"Having been built on the foundation of the apostles and prophets, Christ Jesus Himself being the corner*

stone—just as in Corinth, Paul had laid the foundation teaching of the Lord in Ephesus (as the other apostles and New Testament prophets were also doing elsewhere). That foundation teaching corresponded to what God had done in establishing Christ as the foundation of the spiritual house in heaven. Adhering to this teaching was the basis on which those saints had become part of that house.

- *"In whom the whole* [every] *building, being fitted together, is growing into a holy temple in the Lord"*—the Greek word translated "whole," *"pas,"* is used numerous times in the New Testament and always in the plural, usually translated as "*every.*" This does not refer to a single building, but to several. This translation has led some people to assume that Paul was referring here to the church the Body of Christ, which is not the case. What Paul was describing is that each church of God, as it is properly linked with the others, constitutes the house (temple) of God. The individual disciples as living stones (1 Peter 2:5) were being built together town by town, in churches of God, and together they formed God's house on Earth.
- *"In whom you also are being built together into a dwelling of God in the Spirit"*—he then tells the church in Ephesus that they too were part of that process. There had to be unity of teaching and practice within each church (*"built together,"* verse 22), and also among all the churches *("fitted together,"* verse 21). God could then dwell among them on Earth (the Greek word means a "down-dwelling place")

collectively in the person of the Holy Spirit (in addition to Him residing individually in their bodies).

Ephesians 4:7–16

"But to each one of us grace was given according to the measure of Christ's gift. Therefore it says, 'When He ascended on high, He led captive a host of captives, and He gave gifts to men.' (Now this expression, 'He ascended,' what does it mean except that He also had descended into the lower parts of the earth? He who descended is Himself also He who ascended far above all the heavens, so that He might fill all things.) And He gave some as apostles, and some as prophets, and some as evangelists, and some as pastors and teachers, for the equipping of the saints for the work of service, to the building up of the body of Christ; until we all attain to the unity of the faith, and of the knowledge of the Son of God, to a mature man, to the measure of the stature which belongs to the fullness of Christ.

As a result, we are no longer to be children, tossed here and there by waves and carried about by every wind of doctrine, by the trickery of men, by craftiness in deceitful scheming; but speaking the truth in love, we are to grow up in all aspects into Him who is the head, even Christ, from whom the whole body, being fitted and held together by what every joint supplies, according to the proper working of each individual part, causes the growth of the body for the building up of itself in love."

In this Scripture Paul is describing the process by which living members of the Body of Christ, which he had referred to in chapter 1 as *"the fullness of Him who fills all in all,"* are built up.

Designated men were initially given as gifts to equip the saints for their service, which was intended to bring believers to "*the unity of the faith*" (that is, united adherence to all the teaching of the Lord) and "*of the knowledge of the Son of God*" (that is, united relationship with Christ in all His present capacities on their behalf). In this way all believers would come to experience Christ, not only as their Saviour, but also as their Lord in their obedience, as their Shepherd for receiving direction and care, as their High Priest in their collective worship and service, as their Advocate when they sin, as their Intercessor when they pray, and more.

This goal represents full maturity of believers, which would be arrived at when they were fully developed and fully integrated in mutual support and co-ordinated service according to the commands of the Lord. The full measure of that is the stature of Christ Himself. Therefore, becoming a member of the Body of Christ is not an end in itself, but the beginning of a process designed to bring all members together to full expression of the person of Christ. We have a long way to go.

1 Timothy 3:14,15

"I am writing these things to you, hoping to come to you before long; but in case I am delayed, I write so that you will know how one ought to conduct himself in the household of God, which is the church of the living God, the pillar and support of the truth."

These verses come at the end of the lists of qualities that Paul was giving Timothy for him to look for in men who should be appointed as overseers and deacons in the churches. These churches together constituted the house (sometimes translated *"household"*) of God, and these leadership roles were established by the Lord to govern behaviour in that house. The house is described here as *"the church of the living God."* It is the entire congregation of those called out from the world to be gathered together in local churches, to stand as a testimony to the truth of God. Being in the Body of Christ is based on our confession of Jesus Christ as *"the Son of the living God"* (Matthew 16:16–18), while being gathered together in service and testimony according to the call of God places us in *"the church of the living God."*

Hebrews 3:1–6

"Therefore, holy brethren, partakers of a heavenly calling, consider Jesus, the Apostle and High Priest of our confession; He was faithful to Him who appointed Him, as Moses also was in all His house. For He has been counted worthy of more glory than Moses, by just so much as the builder of the house has more honor than the house. For every house is built by someone, but the builder of all things is God. Now Moses was faithful in all His house as a servant, for a testimony of those things which were to be spoken later; but Christ was faithful as a Son over His house—whose house we are, if we hold fast our confidence and the boast of our hope firm until the end."

Christ is presented in this passage both as the apostle and high priest of our confession. Our confession is what we profess about the truth of God, as taught by Christ. As the apostle, Christ came out from God to confess this truth to mankind. As the priest He has gone back into God's presence to confess it to God on behalf of those who hold it. What is highlighted here is His faithfulness in doing that. A comparison is made to Moses' faithfulness in making the tabernacle exactly as he was told to, because of what it represented, but his status was only that of a servant. Christ's status is that of the son who has all authority over the house of God.

God is building His spiritual house today as disciples are being built into it as "living stones" (1 Peter 2:5). They participate in that as long as they hold fast to their belief in their "hope." That is not referring to the hope of their future salvation, the hope of Christ coming from heaven for them. Rather, it is the reality of Christ being now in heaven which provides the present opportunity of them going in together to God in worship. It is defined in chapter 6:19 ("*a hope both sure and steadfast and one which enters within the veil*") and in 7:19 ("*a better hope, through which we draw near to God*"). Thus, being included in the house of God is a conditional matter and quite distinct, for example, from being in the church the Body of Christ. The faithfulness of both Christ and Moses are highlighted here to stress the need for our faithfulness in doing this.

Hebrews 10:19–25; 12:18–24,28; 13:15

"Therefore, brethren, since we have confidence to enter the holy place by the blood of Jesus, by a new and living way which He inaugurated for us through the veil, that is, His flesh, and since we have a great priest over the house of God, let us draw near with a sincere heart in full assurance of faith, having our hearts sprinkled clean from an evil conscience and our bodies washed with pure

water. Let us hold fast the confession of our hope without wavering, for He who promised is faithful; and let us consider how to stimulate one another to love and good deeds, not forsaking our own assembling together, as is the habit of some, but encouraging one another; and all the more as you see the day drawing near....

For you have not come to a mountain that can be touched and to a blazing fire, and to darkness and gloom and whirlwind, and to the blast of a trumpet and the sound of words which sound was such that those who heard begged that no further word be spoken to them. For they could not bear the command, 'If even a beast touches the mountain, it will be stoned.' And so terrible was the sight, that Moses said, 'I am full of fear and trembling.' But you have come to Mount Zion and to the city of the living God, the heavenly Jerusalem, and to myriads of angels, to the general assembly and church of the firstborn who are enrolled in heaven, and to God, the Judge of all, and to the spirits of the righteous made perfect, and to Jesus, the mediator of a new covenant, and to the sprinkled blood, which speaks better than the blood of Abel....

Therefore, since we receive a kingdom which cannot be shaken, let us show gratitude, by which we may offer to God an acceptable service with reverence and awe.... Through Him then, let us continually offer up a sacrifice of praise to God, that is, the fruit of lips that give thanks to His name."

These Scriptures in Hebrews represent the summit of the epistle. From chapter 1 it climbs through magnificent truths and inescapable reasoning to this climax—"*therefore ... let us draw near.*" This is how we give effect to our holding fast the confession of our hope. We approach God in our spirits, fully assured by faith that we are drawing near in heaven itself, based on the person of Jesus Christ (*"the veil, that is, His flesh"*) and the blood, which He shed and which has been applied to deal for ever with our sins. Unlike the Old Testament worshippers, our hearts have (symbolically) had the blood of Christ applied to them to cleanse our consciences from sin (Hebrews 9:14), and we have been cleansed (symbolically) by *"the washing of water with the word"* (Ephesians 5:26) from all defilement.

In addition, our relationships with each other must be right because this service is collective. We are told to not stop assembling. We gather on Earth to give our spiritual sacrifices audibly (*"the fruit of lips"),* whereby we confess God's name to Him *"so that with one accord you may with one voice glorify the God and Father of our Lord Jesus Christ"* (Romans 15:6). The words in Hebrews 12:28, *"let us show gratitude,"* are translated in the NKJV as *"let us have grace,"* showing that our response to receiving the grace of God in our hearts is to express our appreciation to Him. We do this in an attitude of complete reverence.

Our worship takes place *"in spirit and in truth"* (John 4:24) in heaven, not on Earth, in the place to which we have come - the heavenly city of Jerusalem on the heavenly Mount Zion. Countless worshipping angels are there, as are the souls of believers from the Old and New Testaments who have passed on. God the Father is there on His throne to receive the worship, and Jesus is there as a man, as our mediator. He has made our access to the holy place and our worship possible, on the basis of His shed blood, which satisfies all God's demands.

In contrast, Abel's blood called out to God for revenge (Genesis 4:10); but Christ's blood has brought peace (Colossians 1:20). Just as blood was sprinkled in front of and on the mercy seat in the Old Testament sanctuary (Leviticus 16:14), so it is seen here (symbolically) as being in the sanctuary in heaven for us. This collective worship in God's sanctuary in heaven is the highest service possible for created beings today.

1 Peter 2:1–10

"Therefore, putting aside all malice and all deceit and hypocrisy and envy and all slander, like newborn babies, long for the pure milk of the word, so that by it you may grow in respect to salvation, if you have tasted the kindness of the Lord. And coming to Him as to a living stone which has been rejected by men, but is choice and precious in the sight of God, you also, as living stones, are being built up as a spiritual house for a holy priesthood, to offer up spiritual sacrifices acceptable to God through Jesus Christ. For this is contained in Scripture: 'Behold, I lay in Zion a choice stone, a precious corner stone, and he who believes in Him will not be disappointed.'

This precious value, then, is for you who believe; but for those who disbelieve, 'The stone which the builders rejected, this became the very corner stone,' and, 'a stone of stumbling and a rock of offense'; for they stumble because they are disobedient to the word, and to this doom they were also appointed. But you are a chosen race, a royal priesthood, a holy nation, a people for God's own possession, so that you may proclaim the excellencies of Him who has called you out of darkness into His marvelous light; for you once were not a people, but now you are the people of God; you had not received mercy, but now you have received mercy."

The disciples that Peter was writing to had been born again (1 Peter 1:21,23) and then been built in, as "*living stones,*" to God's spiritual house. This was by means of them coming to Christ as their Lord, not initially for salvation, but continually (as the tense of the verb shows) in obedience to Him. As they engaged in their spiritual service together, the house was continually being built up. Its function was to be a "holy priesthood"—that is, to offer service wholly to God, as one united entity. The job of a high priest is to be an intermediary, to represent the people to God. Christ is our high priest. Through Him, we have access as a priesthood. All believers have a birthright to be priests, but they must be built into the house to function together as the priesthood, because priestly service is collective service.

It is the work of priests to bring sacrifices to God (Hebrews 9:6); they are offered for the people through the high priest (Hebrews 5:1; 13:11). As the holy priesthood, we offer spiritual sacrifices that Christ makes perfect and offers to God on our behalf. The spiritual house has its foundation in heaven in the exalted Christ, who was rejected by men on Earth but glorified by His Father upon His return. This priesthood is also described as being "royal"—literally "a kingdom of priests" (see also Revelation 1:6), just as Israel had been described under the old covenant (Exodus 19:6). It is also described as "a holy nation" and "a people for God's own possession," showing the unity and identity of those who gather in obedience to Him.

Its purpose is to testify to the excellencies of God, who has called them out of spiritual darkness to reveal to them the light of His truth. We see in this passage the linkage between the house of God, the kingdom of God, and the people of God. It was written to people who had been baptized (3:21) and were under the rule of elders (5:1–3), which identifies them as being in churches of God.

Jude verse 3

"Beloved, while I was making every effort to write you about our common salvation, I felt the necessity to write to you appealing that you contend earnestly for the faith which was once for all handed down to the saints."

Jude distinguishes here between the salvation that all believers have in common and "the faith." The faith is the complete body of teaching to be adhered to (see also Appendix B). It includes our common salvation, but also much more. We do not have to contend for our salvation, but we do have to contend for the faith. For example, the apostle Paul said towards the end of his life, "*I have kept the faith*" (2 Timothy 4:7). This body of teaching was originally commanded by the Lord Jesus to His apostles before His ascension to heaven (Acts 1:2). In Matthew 28:18–20, He instructed them to teach the newly baptized disciples *"all that I commanded you."* It was a complete teaching, which was then taught by the apostles to those who believed, becoming known as "*the apostles' teaching*" (Acts 2:42). It was later that it became known as "the faith" (Acts 6:7; 14:22; etc.). By the time Jude wrote this epistle, the faith had been completely passed on to the saints. It was the foundational teaching of the churches. It had been the task of the apostles to put it in place, and it was not to be added to or changed. It is just as relevant and complete today as it was then. We have the great advantage of having it documented for us in the New Testament Scriptures.

Revelation 1:4–6

"John to the seven churches that are in Asia: Grace to you and peace, from Him who is and who was and who is to come, and from the seven Spirits who are before His throne, and from Jesus Christ, the faithful witness, the firstborn of the dead, and the ruler of the kings of the earth. To Him who loves us and released us from our sins by His blood—and He has made us to be a kingdom, priests to His God and Father—to Him be the glory and the dominion forever and ever. Amen."

The apostle John was writing to the seven churches of God that were in Asia Minor. He included, in chapters 2 and 3, specific messages that he was given by the Lord Jesus to each of them. Those churches are described as "lampstands" in verse 20. It was those in the churches that had been made *"a kingdom, priests to His God and Father."* The expression "*kingdom, priests*" is equivalent to the expression "*royal priesthood*" in 1 Peter 2:9 (and corresponds to "*kingdom of priests*" in Exodus 19:6, where it was part of the promise to Israel under the old covenant). It is referring to the kingdom of God, in which Christ is now both king and high priest. The Lord is described here as being among His churches, walking among them (2:1), the same expression that is used in 2 Corinthians 6:16 regarding the temple and people of God. He has authority over these churches. The kingdom, the priesthood, and the house were closely linked under the old covenant, just as they are under the new covenant today.

---

[1] Marriage illustrates this point. God has provided the relationship of marriage for men and women, in which He intends love and intimacy to be expressed. When a husband and wife enter into the position of being a married couple, God joins them, but the ongoing quality of that marriage depends on the love they show within it. Neither intimacy without the commitment of marriage, nor a loveless marriage, fulfills what God designed.

[2] Correspondingly, our spiritual baptism at the time of our salvation is "*by*" Christ (John 1:33), "*in*" the Holy Spirit, "*into*" the Body of Christ (1 Corinthians 12:13).

[3] The quotation is from Leviticus 26:11,12 where it states: *"I will make my dwelling among you..."*. In 2 Corinthians 6:16 it has been changed by the Holy Spirit to: *"I will dwell in* [Greek: 'en'] *them..."*.

Did you love *Discovering True Worship*? Then you should read *Christian Counseling - How to Help Yourself and Others Live Biblically*[1] by Keith Dorricott!

[2]

In this informative book, Keith Dorricott provides many tools to help you to live biblically, and to help others do the same. He explores who we are and why we think and act the way we do, and the negative feelings and emotions, such as anger, guilt and depression, that can arise.

---

1. https://books2read.com/u/3GYZVp
2. https://books2read.com/u/3GYZVp

Together with practical and scriptural advice on how to deal with them, he lays out a framework for how to counsel others from a Christian perspective, with a special focus on specific issues such as marital counseling, crisis counseling and conflict resolution.

Also by Keith Dorricott

The Eternal Purpose: God's Master Plan for the Ages
Our Spiritual Journey
Christian Counseling - How to Help Yourself and Others Live Biblically
Tracing Our Roots - The History of the Churches of God From Pentecost to Today
Uncovering the Pattern: God's Way of Unity For Disciples Today
I Want to Live: The Story of My Battle with Leukemia, My Journey of Discovery, and the Many Who Helped in My Healing
Discovering God's Church
Discovering God's House
Discovering True Worship

www.ingramcontent.com/pod-product-compliance
Lightning Source LLC
Chambersburg PA
CBHW061753020426
42331CB00006B/1467